Hodder Michael Westropp

Prehistoric Phases

Introductory Essays on Prehistoric Archæology

Hodder Michael Westropp

Prehistoric Phases

Introductory Essays on Prehistoric Archæology

ISBN/EAN: 9783742817280

Manufactured in Europe, USA, Canada, Australia, Japa

Cover: Foto ©ninafisch / pixelio.de

Manufactured and distributed by brebook publishing software (www.brebook.com)

Hodder Michael Westropp

Prehistoric Phases

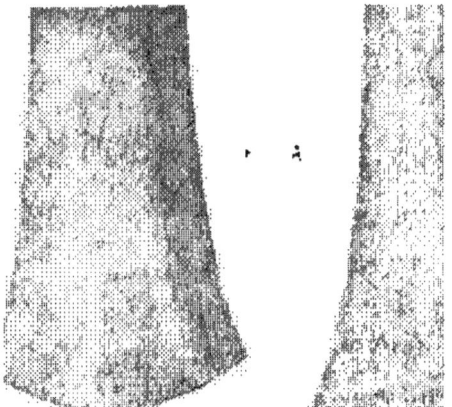

PRE-HISTORIC PHASES.

PRE-HISTORIC PHASES;

OR,

INTRODUCTORY ESSAYS

ON

PRE-HISTORIC ARCHÆOLOGY.

BY

HODDER M. WESTROPP.
AUTHOR OF THE "HANDBOOK OF ARCHÆOLOGY."

WITH ILLUSTRATIONS.

LONDON:
BELL & DALDY, YORK STREET, COVENT GARDEN.
1872.

LONDON:
PRINTED BY WILLIAM CLOWES AND SONS,
STAMFORD STREET AND CHARING CROSS.

TO

SIR JOHN LUBBOCK, Bart.,

THESE PAGES

ARE RESPECTFULLY

DEDICATED.

PREFACE.

THE chapters on Pre-historic Archæology, which form this volume, are chiefly republications, with some additions, of papers read at the Anthropological and Ethnological Societies. I have been induced to publish them in a separate form, as short introductory essays on those subjects, which have lately excited much attention in Pre-historic Archæology. To Mr. Norgate I am indebted for a good many of the illustrative woodcuts. My thanks are due to Mr. Murray for electros of the carvings at Lough Crew; and to Mr. Day for the woodcuts of his unique example of an Irish bronze sword. Through the kindness of Albert Way, Esq., I am able to insert woodcuts of some examples of Italian celts in my collection, and which have been engraved by the

Archæological Institute. The Royal Irish Academy has allowed me only a very small portion of the woodcuts in its catalogue. The Publishers have kindly permitted me to introduce some of the woodcuts from Demmin's "Weapons of War;" also to insert the lithograph of rock-carvings, from Mr. Brett's "Guiana."

H. M. W.

Ventnor, 1872.

INTRODUCTION.

A NEW science has dawned upon us, lighting up the earliest history of mankind. Pre-historic archæology is the latest to arrive of a series of luminaries that have dispelled the mist of ages, and replaced time-honoured traditions by scientific truths. The silent past has been made to speak, and the sea of unrecorded ages to render up its dead. Long buried things have become witnesses of the deeds and modes of life in the remotest times. Pre-historic archæology has opened up a long vista through distant historic periods, to the farthest and darkest ages. It has been defined as the history of men, and things that have no history.

All over the world are scattered vestiges and relics of unknown races and times, of races which existed in times before history commenced. As Dr. Wilson observes, "The investigation of the underlying chronicles of Europe's most ancient human history, has placed beyond question that its historic period was preceded by an unhistoric one of long duration, marked by a slow progression from arts of the rudest kind, to others which involved the germs of all later development."

The first appearance of man on the globe, hitherto supposed to be of late date, has been thrown back to a remote period. Until the last few years, the earliest records of man lay hidden in the earth, and the earliest witnesses of his labours, the works of his own hands, were passed over unheeded. We have now indisputable evidence that man has outlived vast changes of climate, and has seen race after race of animals disappear around him, the mammoth, the elk, the reindeer, the gigantic bear. The late discoveries in pre-historic archæology confirm, in the most unequivocal manner, the high antiquity of the human race. In the remotest ages, which historic traditions mention, we find that man had already reached a certain stage of intellectual and moral development, but, before attaining that point, he passed during many ages through a series of intermediate stages, between a mere animal existence, and the first phase of civilization. History being silent on this period, of which even approximately we cannot calculate the immense duration, it is to prehistoric archæology we are indebted for revealing its secrets. Everything relative to the earliest dawnings of human life demands the attention of every one, who devotes his mind to the great problem of our origin, and of the laws which govern the evolution of our race on the surface of the globe.

To sum up in the words of a late writer in the "Edinburgh Review," "Pre-historic archæology tells us, that in Europe there has been a steady progress in the usages and appliances of social life. Man first appeared on the scene as a savage, living by the chase. Then a race of shepherds and tillers of the earth come before us, the introducers of domestic animals into Europe; then the knowledge of bronze gradually crept northwards, and a commerce by barter sprang up; and lastly, a knowledge of iron, and a commerce carried on by means of a coinage. Thus we are conducted gradually from the remote geological past, to the borders of history in north and central Europe."

In the following chapters we have attempted to trace the sequence of stages in the development of man, during pre-historic times, and also of the works of his hands from the earliest and rudest ages up to that period when the progressive development of man and his works, reached its maturity. A necessary sequence in the phases of man's social development, and in the stages of the progressive improvement in his works, appears to be an invariable law.

I have added chapters on Cromlechs and Rock Carvings, as they belong to pre-historic times, and may be considered as the result and products of the rude development and semi-civilization of pre-historic phases.

CONTENTS.

I.
On the Earliest Phases of Civilization 1

II.
On the Degraded Phase 37

III.
On the Sequence of Stone, Bronze, and Iron Implements. 40

IV.
On the Sequence of Phases of Civilization, and Contemporaneous Implements. 99

V.
On the Analogous Forms of Implements among Early and Primitive Races 115

VI.
On the Tribal System 127

VII.
Cromlechs 143

VIII.
Rock Carvings 176

DESCRIPTION OF PLATE I.

FLINT ARROW-HEADS AND SPEAR-HEADS.

ENGLAND.
1. Flint arrow-head, barbed. *Half-size.*
2 & 3. Flint arrow-heads, leaf-shaped. In my collection. *Half-size.*

DENMARK.
4. Flint spear-head. *One-third size.*
5. Flint arrow-head, barbed.
6. Flint arrow-head, triangular. In my collection. } *Half-size.*

IRELAND.
7. Flint arrow-head, leaf-shaped.
8. Flint arrow-head, barbed.
9. Flint arrow-head, triangular.
14. Flint spear-head. In my collection. } *Half-size.*

ITALY.
10.
11. } Flint arrow-heads, stemmed. In my collection. *Half-size.*
12.
13. Flint arrow-head. In Castellani collection. *Half-size.*

FRANCE.
16. Flint arrow-head, barbed. *Half-size.*
15.
17. } Flint arrow-heads, stemmed. In my collection. *Half-size.*
18.

SWITZERLAND.
19.
20. } Flint arrow-heads, stemmed. *Half-size.*
21. Arrow-head of crystal. From St. Aubin, Neufchatel. In my collection. *Half-size.*

NORTH AMERICA.
  22. } Flint arrow-heads, stemmed. In my collection. *Half-*
  23. } *size.*
JAPAN.
  24. Arrow-head of grey chalcedony, triangular.
  25. Arrow-head of jasper.   } *Stemmed.*
  26. Arrow-head. Christy Museum.   } *Half-size.*
CHALDÆA.
  27. Flint arrow-head. Berlin Museum. *One-fifth size.*
EGYPT.
  28. Flint arrow-head. Berlin Museum. *One-sixth size.*
CAPE OF GOOD HOPE.
  29. Arrow-head of quartzite, leaf-shaped. In my collection. *Half-size.*
PERU.
  30. Arrow-head of quartzite, stemmed.
  31. Arrow-head of quartzite. In the Museum of Queen's College, Cork. *Half-size.*
MEXICO.
  32. } Arrow-heads of obsidian, stemmed. From Tylor's
  33. } "Anahuac." *Half-size.*
GREENLAND.
  34. Arrow-head of chert, stemmed. In Mr. Day's collection. *One-third size.*
TIERRA DEL FUEGO.
  35. Arrow-head of flint, stemmed. From Nilsson's "Stone Age." *Actual size.*
ALGIERS.
  36. Arrow-head of flint, stemmed. Christy Museum. *One-fourth size.*
EASTER ISLAND.
  37. Arrow-head of obsidian. Anthropological Institute. *One-fourth size.*

DESCRIPTION OF PLATE II.

STONE IMPLEMENTS.

1. EGYPT.—Celt of jade. In the Christy Museum. 1¾ inches.
2. GREECE.—Celt of diorite. In Mr. Finlay's collection. 6¼ inches.
3. ITALY.—Celt of diorite. In the Castellani collection. 5 inches.
4. CHALDÆA.—Celt of basalt. In the British Museum. 2 inches.
5. INDIA.—Celt, from Bundelkund. In my collection. 4 inches.
6. JAPAN.—Celt of greenish stone. In the Christy Museum. 2⅞ inches.
7. PEGU.—Celt of greenish stone. In Colonel Lane Fox's collection.
8. CHINA.—Celt of green jade. In the Christy Museum. 2⅞ inches.
9. ENGLAND.—Celt of flint. In my collection. 4¼ inches.
10. IRELAND.—Celt of flint. In my collection. 4⅞ inches.
11. DENMARK.—Celt of flint. In my collection. 4¼ inches.
12. FRANCE.—From Chateau-Dun. In my collection. 5 inches.
13. SPAIN.—From Genista Cave, Gibraltar. In the Christy Museum. 4½ inches.
14. RUSSIA.—From Minsk. In the International Exhibition, Paris. 4¼ inches.
15. GERMANY.—Celt of flint.—In my collection. 5 inches.
16. ALGERIA.—Celt of flint.—In the Christy Museum. 2¼ inches.
17. NORTH AMERICA.—Celt of flint. In my collection. 4¼ inches.
18. MEXICO.—From Dr. Wilson's "Pre-historic Man," 4½ inches.
19. PERU.—From Cuzco. In my collection. 3¼ inches.
20. BRAZIL.—Brought by Captain Burton. In the Anthropological Institute. 6 inches.
21. NEW ZEALAND.—Celt of jade. In my collection. 7½ inches.
22. NEW CALEDONIA.—Celt of jade. In my collection. 6½ inches.
23. ST. DOMINGO.—Carib celt of coarse jade, with carved face. In my collection. 8 inches.
24. AUSTRALIA.—Celt of basalt. In my collection. 6 inches.

DESCRIPTION OF PLATE III.

BRONZE ARROW-HEADS AND SPEAR-HEADS.

1. German arrow-head. Museum of Sigmaringen. From Demmin's "Weapons of War," p. 130.
2. Arrow-head, with tang. Found in Mecklenburg. Schwerin Museum. From "Horæ Ferales," pl. vi. $2\frac{7}{8}$ inches long.
3. Arrow, or javelin-head of leaf-shape. Found in Mecklenburg. Schwerin Museum. From "Horæ Ferales," pl. vi. $4\frac{1}{4}$ inches long. Both the above are evident copies of the flint arrow or spear-heads.
4. Barbed arrow-head. Berlin Museum. From "Horæ Ferales," pl. vi. This is also a copy of a flint barbed arrow-head. $1\frac{7}{10}$ inches long.
5. German arrow-head. Museum of Sigmaringen. From Demmin's "Weapons of War," p. 130.
6. Egyptian arrow-head. From Sir G. Wilkinson's "Ancient Egyptians," vol. i. p. 353.
7. Arrow-head from France. Museum of the Louvre. From Demmin's "Weapons of War," p. 135.
8. German arrow-head. Museum of Sigmaringen. From Demmin's "Weapons of War," p. 130.
9. German arrow-head. Museum of Sigmaringen. From Demmin's "Weapons of War," p. 130.
10. Arrow-head, from France. Louvre. From Demmin's "Weapons of War," p. 135.
11. Greek spear-head.
12. Javelin-head. Hanover Museum. From "Horæ Ferales," pl. vi. $4\frac{3}{4}$ inches long.
13. Javelin-head. Ireland. British Museum. From "Horæ Ferales," pl. vi. $4\frac{1}{4}$ inches long.
14. Spear-head. Ireland. "Catalogue of the Royal Irish Academy," p. 499.
15. Javelin-head. Ireland. British Museum. From "Horæ Ferales," pl. vi. $4\frac{1}{4}$ inches long.

16. Javelin-head. France. Hotel de Cluny, Paris. From "Horæ Ferales," pl. vi. 4¾ *inches long*.
17. Spear-head. Probably Irish. British Museum. From "Horæ Ferales," pl. vi. 10½ *inches long*.
18. Spear-head. This fine weapon was found with a hoard of bronzes, at Dowris, King's County, Ireland. There are several spear-heads of this type in the Museum of the Royal Irish Academy. See Sir W. Wilde's "Catalogue," p. 499. British Museum. From "Horæ Ferales," pl. vi. 14 *inches long*.
19. Plain spear-head. Found in the Thames. British Museum. From "Horæ Ferales," pl. vi. 13¼ *inches long*.
20. Leaf-shaped spear-head. Hanover Museum. From "Horæ Ferales," pl. vi. 9¼ *inches long*.

DESCRIPTION OF PLATE IV.

1, 2, 3. Flat celts. In my collection.
4, 5, 6, 7. Palstaves. In my collection.
    Showing the development of the palstave from the flat celt.

DESCRIPTION OF PLATE V.

STONE CIRCLES.

1. Single Stone Circle. Jewurgi. From Waring's "Stone Monuments," pl. 63, fig. 5.
2. Double Stone Circle. Jewurgi. Waring's "Stone Monuments," pl. 63, fig. 6.
3. Stone Circle. Algeria. From Flowers' "Pre-historic Sepulchres of Algeria."
4. Enclosure of Upright Stones. Doh-ayeb, Persia. Waring, pl. 60, fig. 3.
5. Double Stone Circle. Abury. Waring, pl. 38, fig. 1.

6. A Scandinavian tumulus, with a Single Stone Circle. Waring, pl. 32, fig. 1.
7. Tumulus. Near Lough Corrib, Ireland. With Double Stone Circle. From Sir W. Wilde's "Lough Corrib."
8. Cromlech. Tarf, Algeria. With Stone Circle. From Flowers' "Algeria."
9. Cromlech. Abury. With Stone Circle. Waring, pl. 38, fig. 1.
10. Great Stone Circle. Brogar, Orkney. Waring, pl. 48, fig. 8.
11. Stonehenge. Restored.

DESCRIPTION OF PLATE VI.

Timehri, or carved rocks. On the River Carentyn. From Rev. W. H. Brett's "Indian Tribes of Guiana."

DESCRIPTION OF THE WOODCUTS.

1. Rude flint implement. From the gravel drift at Hoxne. After Frere. "Archæologia," 1800, pl. xv. From Sir John Lubbock's "Pre-historic Times," p. 337. *One-half actual size.*
2. Another specimen. After Frere. "Archæologia," 1800, pl. xv. From Sir John Lubbock's "Pre-historic Times," p. 336.
3. Stone implement. From Madras. From Sir John Lubbock's "Pre-historic Times," p. 340.
4. Flint core, from which flakes have been struck off. Ireland. "Catalogue of the Royal Irish Academy," p. 6.
5. Flint flake. Denmark. From Sir John Lubbock's "Pre-historic Times," p. 81. *Actual size.*
6. Arrow-shaped flake. From Ireland. It is worked at the butt end. "Catalogue of the Royal Irish Academy," p. 72.
7. Flint flake. Denmark. From Sir John Lubbock's "Pre-historic Times," p. 80.
8. Australian flake. From Sir John Lubbock's "Pre-historic Times," p. 84. *One-half actual size.*
9. Pressigny core. From Demmin's "Weapons of War," p. 78.
10. Triangular flint arrow-head. "Catalogue of the Royal Irish Academy," p. 19. *Actual size.*
11. Indented flint arrow-head. "Catalogue of the Royal Irish Academy," p. 20. *Actual size.*
12. Barbed flint arrow-head. "Catalogue of the Royal Irish Academy," p. 22. *Actual size.*
13. Leaf-shaped flint arrow-head, showing the gradual passage into the spear-head. "Catalogue of the Royal Irish Academy. *Actual size.*

14. Flint axe. Denmark. Ground at the edge. Showing the initial stage in celt making. From Sir John Lubbock's "Pre-historic Times," p. 94.
15. Danish flint hatchet, chipped at edge. From Dammin's "Weapons of War," p. 78.
16. Stone celt or hatchet. Ireland. Ground all over. "Catalogue of the Royal Irish Academy," p. 41. 5¾ *inches long, and* 2 *broad.*
17. Stone celt, with a wooden handle. Monaghan, Ireland. "Catalogue of Royal Irish Academy," p. 46.
18. Stone celt, with wooden handle. Concise; from Dosor. From Sir John Lubbock's "Pre-historic Times," p. 89. *One-third actual size.*
19. Copper arrow or spear-head, hammered into shape. Cincinnati. Whittlesey, "Boston Society of Natural History," vol. i. pl. 16, fig. 0. From Sir John Lubbock's "Pre-historic Times," p. 245. *One-third actual size.*
20. Copper celt, from Ireland, cast. "Catalogue of the Royal Irish Academy," p. 368. *One-half actual size.*
21. Greek sword. Museum of Artillery, Paris. 32 *inches long.*
22. Roman sword. 26 *inches long.*
23. Roman sword. 23 *inches long.*
24. Danish sword. Copenhagen Museum. 37 *inches long.*
25. German sword. Museum of Cassel. 22 *inches long.*
26. Danish sword. Copenhagen Museum. 35 *inches long.*
27. British sword. Tower of London.
28. } Irish swords. Meyrick Collection. From Dammin's
29. } "Weapons of War."
30. Irish bronze sword, with bone handle. In the collection of R. Day, Esq., F.S.A. 25 *inches long.*
31. } The three principal types of bronze celts, and the manner
32. } in which they are supposed to have been handled. "Cat-
33. } alogue of the Royal Irish Academy," p. 367.
34. French bronze palstave. Found in the Seine. Museum of Artillery, Paris.
35. Danish bronze palstave. Copenhagen Museum. 11 *inches long.*
36. German bronze palstave. Museum of Sigmaringen. 6 *inches long.*

German bronze palstave. Museum of Hanover. The last from woodcuts, from Demmin's "Weapons of War."
37. Socketed celt. Ireland. "Catalogue of the Royal Irish Academy," p. 385. *One-third actual size.*
38. Socketed celt. Denmark. From Sir John Lubbock's "Pre-historic Times," p. 26. *One-third actual size.*
39. Socketed celt. France. In my collection. *5 inches long.*
40. Socketed celt. Switzerland. Museum of Geneva. The last two from Demmin's "Weapons of War," p. 144.
41. Half of a celt mould. From Ireland. It is of mica slate, *6¾ inches long, by 4 wide*, and presents upon the surface the apertures by the means of which it was adjusted by the other half. "Catalogue of the Royal Irish Academy," p. 91.
42. Flat bronze celt. From the South of Italy.
43. Bronze palstave, or winged celt. From Perugia.
44. Bronze palstave, or winged celt. From South of Italy.
45. Bronze socketed celt. From the South of Italy. These four Italian celts are in my collection. The woodcuts have been lent by the Archæological Institute, through Albert Way, Esq. *Half-size.*
46. Six German arrow-heads, iron. Museum of Sigmaringen.
47. Palstave of iron. Collection of M. Az. Lintz.
Palstave of iron. National Museum of Munich. *7½ inches long.*
48. Spear-head of iron. Found at Selzen, Hesse. *16 inches long.*
Spear-head of iron. Found at Londinières. Museum of Artillery, Paris. From Demmin's "Weapons of War," p. 154. *15 inches long.*
49. German sword, the blade of iron, the hilt of bronze. From Hallstadt. *16½ inches long.*
50. German socketed celt, of iron. Cabinet of Antiquities, Vienna. *15 inches long.*
51. Stone Circle. Denmark. From Sir John Lubbock's "Pre-historic Times," p. 105.
52. Kit's Coty House, near Maidstone. From Sir John Lubbock's "Pre-historic Times," p. 107.
53. Indian Dolmen. After Colonel Meadows Taylor. From Sir John Lubbock's "Pre-historic Times," p. 121.

DESCRIPTION OF WOODCUTS.

54. Primitive Tomb. Acora, Peru. From Squier's "Primeval Monuments of Peru," p. 5.
55. Intihuanas (Sun Circles) of Sillustani. Peru. From Squier's "Primeval Monuments of Peru," p. 15.
56. Carved Stones, in Cairn. Lough Crew, Ireland. From Fergusson's "Rude Stone Monuments," p. 216.
57. Sculptured rock. Forsyth County, Georgia, North America. From New York "Anthropological Journal," No. 1.
58. Figure drawn on the wall by boys in Italy. From Hobhouse's "Illustrations to the Fourth Canto of Childe Harold."
59. Ausam. Arab tribal tokens or signs. From Finn's "Byeways of Palestine," p. 32.

INSTRUCTIONS TO THE BINDER.

PLATES.

	PAGE
I. FLINT ARROW-HEADS	58
II. STONE CELTS	66
III. BRONZE ARROW-HEADS	78
IV. BRONZE PALSTAVES	86
V. STONE CIRCLES	160
VI. CARVED ROCKS, GUIANA	182

TABULATION of the STAGES of DEVELOPMENT of MAN and IMPLEMENTS.

Stages of the development of Man.	Stages of the development of Implements.		Contemporaneous Animals.	Contemporaneous Trees in Denmark.	Contemporaneous Burials.
Barbarous	Palæolithic	Rough Flints.	Mammoth. Rhinoceros Tichorinus. Cave Bear, Hyæna. Reindeer.		
Hunting	Mesolithic	{ Flint Flakes. Flints chipped into shape.	Red Deer. Wild Boar. Wild Ox.	} Fir.	Tumuli. Stone circles. Body in a sitting posture.
Pastoral	Neolithic	{ Stone implements ground at edge. Stone implements all ground and polished.	Sheep. Ox. Goat.		Cromlechs Stone circles. Body in a contracted posture.
Agricultural	Bronze	{ Arrow-heads. Spear-heads. Swords. Flat celts. Palstaves. Socketed celts.	{ Sheep. Ox. Horse. Pig. } Domesticated Cereals. { Wheat Barley	Oak.	Tumuli. Cremation.
State	Iron	{ Celts. Spears, swords. Arrow-heads.		Beech.	Tumuli. Cremation. Inhumation.

PRE-HISTORIC PHASES.

ON THE EARLIEST PHASES OF CIVILIZATION.

As it is in the nature of the development of man, as an individual and collectively, to be progressive, it must of necessity follow that this development should be from a lower to a higher stage, from the weak, helpless state of infancy, to the maturity and power of manhood; from a rude and barbarous phase to a more refined civilization. The idea itself of progression involves the belief in an ascent from lower to higher.

The individual man begins life as a helpless infant, then rises through the successive stages of childhood, youth, till he reaches maturity in manhood.

The initial steps of man's social progress, are those of a rude and barbarous savage, thence advancing through successive phases, society attains a more perfect and complete form. Adopting the words of

Waitz, "We may start from the assumption that, as in the life of individuals, so also in that of nations, all cultivation is something secondary, resting upon a gradual progress to a better state than was the primitive or natural state of mankind. This natural state, marked by the absence of all cultivation, we must imagine to have been the original condition of every race."

Man collectively is led by a natural instinct, which is shared in common by all the higher races of men, to follow out a similar sequence of phases of civilization, as naturally as the growth of the individual man proceeds in the same stages of development.

This upward development is the necessary result of the inherent and peculiar progressive power and improvable nature of man, acting in obedience to the dictates of a mental impulse, peculiar to the higher races, which compels him to fill his destined course. As Dr. Wilson observes, "Civilization is for man development. It is self-originated; it matures all the faculties natural to him, and is progressive and seemingly ineradicable."

It appears as if there were but one history for every separate people, one uniform process of development for every race, each passing through successive phases, before attaining its highest social development; for every race must pass through the necessary transitional stages before it can arrive at a higher development.

These successive phases are the rude and barbarous, the hunting, the pastoral, and the agricultural, corresponding with, and analogous to, the stages of infancy, childhood, youth, manhood in the individual man. This sequence is invariable in man, as an individual and collectively.

Man in the earliest stage of his development, like the helpless infant, was equally naked, both as to body and mind. Like other animals, without speech, without experience of the past, without knowledge of the future, without any idea of a superior being, he wandered through wilds and forests, guided and governed solely by the instincts of his nature. His earliest dwellings were mountain caves. In the words of Horace, quoted by Sir Charles Lyell, and on which he makes these remarks, "They who in later times have embraced a similar theory, have been led to it by no deference to the opinion of their pagan predecessors, but rather in spite of very strong prepossessions in favour of an opposite hypothesis."
"When animals, Horace says, first crept forth from the newly-formed earth, a dumb and filthy herd, they

fought for acorns and lurking places with their nails and fists, then with clubs, and at last with arms, which, taught by experience, they had forged. They then invented names for things, and words to express their thoughts, after which they begun to desist from war, to fortify cities, and enact laws." Sir Charles Lyell further observes: "The opinion entertained generally by the classical writers of Greece and Rome, that man in the first stage of his existence was but just removed from the brutes, is faithfully expressed by Horace in the above lines. The picture of transmutation given in those verses, however severe and contemptuous the strictures lavishly bestowed on it by Christian commentators, accords singularly with the train of thought which the modern doctrine of progressive development has encouraged."

As a recent writer observes, however humiliating it may be to our pride, we must acknowledge that, in the earliest period of his existence, man was scarcely distinguishable from the brute. The desire to supply his wants absorbed his whole thoughts. All his efforts tended to one single aim, to obtain his daily food.

All evidence tends to prove the original barbarous state of mankind; but man, like an upstart, in the pride of his matured intellect, in the pride of his acquired position, ignores his low and base origin.

From the late discoveries in pre-historic archæology, primitive man, the cotemporary of the mammoth and the cave bear, has been proved by his implements and weapons, and by the traces of his mode of life, to have been a savage of the lowest grade; a dweller in caves and rock shelters, and, like the Fuegian, when first discovered, rather a beast than a man, tearing human bodies to pieces and eating the flesh raw and bloody. He fed on wild fruits, or devoured raw fish, or fought with his fellow men, or with the brutes for the carcases killed by them. Not content with the flesh of the animals he had killed, he split up the bones and sucked the marrow contained in them. His weapons were of the rudest kind, large flint hatchets, such as have been found in the gravel drift of the valleys of the Somme, and the Ouse. His life was a continual state of warfare. He fought for everything, for food, for women. Among the degraded aboriginal tribes of North America the men fought for the possession of the women, like stags, or the males of other wild beasts. Horace describes primitive men in similar terms. "Venerem incertam rapientes more ferarum;" and from the analogies of those degraded tribes of North America we have no reason to question this description.

Some African tribes in a similar savage state, are described by Sir Samuel Baker, as mere apes, trusting entirely to the productions of nature for their subsistence, and as far below the brutes.

Mr. Anderson ("Okovango," p. 131) makes a similar remark in regard to some other African tribes. "Human nature," he says, "seemed lower than that of the brute creation, whilst at the same time almost diabolical."

Of this earliest barbarous stage the Veddahs, of Ceylon, afford a further example; they live more or less by hunting, and the use of the bow; they dwell in caves, or under the shelter of overhanging rocks. They subsist upon roots, grain, and fruit, when they can procure them; and upon birds, bats, crows, owls, and kites, which they bring down with the bow. They have no knowledge of a God, nor of a future state; no instinct of worship except some addiction to ceremonies analogous to devil worship, so degraded are they, that it has appeared doubtful in certain cases, whether they possess any language whatever, their communication with one another being made by signs, grimaces, and guttural sounds, which have little or no resemblance to distinct words or systematic language.* Such must have been the cave dwellers of England and Belgium; such the inmates of the caves of Dordogne, which establish evidence of man in an analogous barbarous stage.

Humboldt, when remarking the savage and brutal state of the Indians at Pararuma, on the Orinoco, is obliged to admit that such was the primitive character of our species. "The assemblage of Indians," he says, "at Pararuma, again excited in us that interest, which everywhere attaches man in a cultivated state to the study of man, in a savage condition. How difficult to recognize in this infancy of society, in this assemblage of dull, silent, inanimate Indians, the *primitive character of our species.* Human nature does not here manifest those features of artless simplicity, of which poets in every language have drawn such enchanting pictures. The savage of the Orinoco appeared to us as hideous as the savage of the Mississippi." †

* See Sir Emerson Tennant's "Ceylon."

† Much confusion arises from considering the terms "natural state" and "state of nature" as synonomous, a mistake made by Lord Shaftesbury, and by Archbishop Whately. A state of nature is when man is in a savage, uncivilized, barbarous, and primitive state, before he has taken his initial steps towards civilization.

Man is in his natural state when endowed with the high physical organization and progressive intellect given to him by nature, and when placed in a position to which he is fitted by it.

HUNTING PHASE.

Man, emerging slowly and gradually from the primitive and barbarous stage, becomes a nomadic hunter and fisher. Unacquainted with every art but the imperfect one of fabricating, in a rude manner, arms and implements for the chase, dependent on chance alone, and the seasons for the means of satisfying his wants. Living in a wild and uncultivated state, when his means of sustenance were too few and too precarious, man became a hunter from necessity, nomadic in his habits, and obliged to dispute his life with men, who, like himself, were scarcely less savage than the beasts of the forest. As has been said, "Man is eminently a hunting animal, but there is no prey which he follows with such zest and perseverance as his fellow man." A hunter is a

---

The rude Australian typifies the first, the Apollo Belvedere the latter.

A plant, uncultivated in the wilds of nature, is in a state of nature; the same plant, highly cultivated in a conservatory, is in its natural state.

Man in a high state of civilisation, is in a natural state, but cannot be said to be in a state of nature.

We may therefore thus briefly distinguish, man in a state of nature is man, minus civilisation. Man in his natural state is man, plus civilization.

wild man, his food is wild game; he lives as the
tiger lives, catching his prey by his superior cunning,
strength, and pluck. The flesh of that prey is his
food, the skin of that prey is his mantle. He is a
companion of wild beasts, and his only art is how to
seize and kill them. He may not build a house,
he may not till the ground; he may not tarry in one
place, for the wild game which he procures is always
flying from his poisoned arrow and his plunging
knife; and the law of his existence chains him to the
buffalo track. His hand is lifted against everything
that lives. Such is the prairie hunter. In this stage
the progress of man must have been extremely slow,
as we have evidence among the American Indians.
Man's natural instincts predominating in this phase,
it was necessarily stationary and unprogressive.
His intellect was dormant, but once awakened, his
progress was onward and upward.

THE PASTORAL PHASE.

As man advances, becoming conscious of the sustenance afforded by the animals he has tamed, and
which he has learned to preserve, domesticate, and
multiply: he becomes a shepherd, a herdsman, but to
a certain extent continues a nomad, wandering with

his flocks and herds wherever pasture or security invites. "A herdsman is a tame man, his food is milk and cheese, the flesh of goats and of calves. He has to provide for his wants by knowledge, care, and kindness. The cow yields him milk, and the goat yields him cloth; yet he wins these requisites from them, not by murderous cunning, but by tender love. He surrounds himself with a world of helpless creatures, goats and horses, sheep and cattle; creatures for whom he has to think by night, and watch by day. When the hunter sharpens his blade, the herdsman has to sharpen his wits, if he would thrive in his acts and increase his flocks. Such a man is the Bedouin Arab." A slow transitional mode of life becomes necessary to pass from the irregular and changeable activity of the hunting, to the uniform industry of the agricultural phase.

The first step from savage towards civil life among all races, is the division into tribes, of either the family, or of the clan. The tribal system is the first stage into which human society is moulded, or, to use Mr. Dixon's words,* the oldest form in which men were organized into societies was division into tribes. It arises from the condition and necessities of the earliest wanderers. It is the prevailing system

* "New America."

among pastoral nations. Most nations may be traced back to this primitive form. The tribe system is a development of the family. The first wanderer from the original seat of his people, strays forth into foreign lands at the head of his family; the father is at once the priest, the judge, and the king. He rules his children, as the ablest and the wisest; round the original family gather their slaves and dependents, all the members of the original family and their followers form a single political unit. No individual has an existence, except as a member of this body. Their flocks and herds form a common property. They possess no clear idea of individual ownership. This state of things among pastoral nations is vividly brought before us in the Scriptural accounts of Lot and Abraham. This system prevailed in many countries, it is found in Media and India, in Mesopotamia, Arabia, and Scythia, among all wandering and pastoral nations. It is found in America, and has existed in Ireland in the early periods. Mr. Richey justly observes: " So essentially similar are the ideas of all nations on this early state of society, that the difficulties in understanding the Irish tribal system, are often cleared up by an examination of the village laws of India, or the village communities of Russia."

AGRICULTURAL PHASE.

In the further progress of his development, keeping pace with the progress of his mental powers and capacities; when no longer content with the fruit and plants which chance throws in his way, man learns to form a stock of them, to collect them around him, to sow, to plant them, to favour their reproduction by the labour of culture, he becomes stationary and devotes himself to agriculture.* "A genial climate, an easily cultivated soil, bountiful in indigenous fruits, would enable him not only to make his permanent abode, but to devote a portion of his time to the improvement of his superior nature. He tires of his wandering life, he builds sheds for his cattle, and lays up stores of fodder in barns; he burns a tract

* We must however admit what Mr. Baring Gould very justly observes. "Those divisions are not however absolute, for, perhaps, there never was a time when people did not make some rude attempts at tillage, and domestication of animals. Among the refuse of lacustrine villages, which belong to a remote period, the discovery of grain and bones gnawed by dogs, proves that, as far back as man can be traced, there are indications of his having attempted both.

So also agricultural races have indulged occasionally in the pursuit of game, or have set apart a caste to hunt and fish, and fight, whilst the bulk of the people tilled the soil.—*Origin and Development of Religious Belief*, vol. i. p. 190.

of forest land, and sows corn in the ashes. His first *field* is a place where the trees are felled, a clearing in the forest, and his first plough a hoe. Thus the nomad becomes an agriculturist, and takes a more stable position. The movable tent gives place to a permanently fixed dwelling; the tilled corn fields yield a richer harvest the more they are cultivated; the forests surrounding his home give him fuel and building materials; the fields provide him with grass and winter fodder for his cattle, and even the waters yield him tribute. The owner cultivates and guards his territory, he has devoted all his care and labour to it, it is his *own*, he *will* and *ought* to possess it for himself, and for his descendants. Other agriculturists settle in his neighbourhood; each builds his own dwelling house, tills his own ground, and appropriates to himself the territory which he requires; territories are laid out, landmarks between properties are set up; the right of possession becomes more defined, and comprises also the landed territory. The patriarchal life ceases, every landowner' becomes a man for himself."*

Agriculture may be considered as the most important step in the development of civilization, it is indeed the basis of all civilization. An agricultural public offers greater facilities for civilization

* Nilsson's " Primitive Inhabitants of Scandinavia."

than hunting and pastoral tribes. We may quote the following passage from Sir Gardner Wilkinson, which shows how agriculture gives an impetus to the progress of a people, and renders it superior to all others. "The state of the hunter and the shepherd differ widely from the agriculturist. In the former the wants of each member of society depend entirely upon his individual exertions; and since no time can be spared for industrious employment at home, civilization can make little or no progress, and arts remain totally unknown. The shepherd indeed possesses some advantages over the hunter, but still he has neither the means nor the inclination to arise from that primitive state which contents itself with merely satisfying the common wants of man; and if he attempts a predatory warfare against a neighbouring tribe, his conquests are confined to the pillage or desolation of the invaded territory. But when agriculture enables man to produce an abundant supply of the necessaries of life, always keeping pace in a favourable soil, with the increase of population, property becomes established and defined, emulation succeeds, and arts and civilization are rapidly introduced. The labours of the few, besides satisfying their own wants, are found sufficient to maintain those members of society who are employed in other occupations; and hence arises that distinction of agricultural and other classes, which were at so early a period introduced into the fertile regions of Egypt and India."*

The succeeding stage of his development is when, having acquired property in flocks, and in land which he has cleared and cultivated, and being anxious to secure quiet possession of what he had gained by his labour, conventions, tacit or expressed, were introduced, and became the rule of the actions of individuals, the measure of their claims, and the law of their reciprocal relations, thus, an organized society was evolved. "Labour was divided among its various members. Different professions (sometimes *ranks* so called) arose. Some men occupied themselves in tilling the ground, working the mines, managing the flocks, &c., others sold superfluities, and procured what is wanting by means of barter, or trade with other communities and districts; others again defend the property of the community against foreign and domestic foes; and lastly, others promote intelli-

* Sir Gardner Wilkinson's "Topography of Thebes," p. ix. We must remark that these phases are not always synchronous in all countries. Nations are often found side by side in different phases of civilization. The Hebrews, a pastoral people, rich in flocks and herds, were frequently compelled by want to seek corn in Egypt, a nation then far advanced in a high state of civilization.

gence, education, and the cultivation of mind, and a governor or chief is elected to watch over the whole, and to secure and guarantee the right of all."* Law and government were thus gradually evolved; these once established, the progress of the development of man increased rapidly towards that highest stage, when it reached that mature state and highest degree of culture, which culminated in the periods of high civilization in Egypt, Babylon, Nineveh, India, and at later periods in Greece, Rome, and lately in the more perfect refinement of England and France.

We shall now adduce some evidences of the different races of men in their several phases of civilization, or stages of development.

Of the lowest, rude, and barbarous stage, travellers have given us frequent proofs in their description of races which they have found in the most degraded state, and which may be considered as representative types of man in his earliest phase.

Of the existence of this barbarous phase in the initial period of man's development, we have the following evidence.

The rude implements discovered in the valley of

* Nilsson's "Primitive Inhabitants of Scandinavia."

the Somme, in France, at Hoxne, Santon Downham, Thetford, in England, in conjunction with elephant remains, and those of other extinct animals, raises a presumption that the men who made them were themselves rude and barbarous.

From the discoveries in the valley of the Somme, Sir John Lubbock draws the following conclusion: " Along the banks of the rivers ranged a savage race, and in the forests wandered the mammoth, the two-horned woolly rhinoceros, a species of lion, the musk ox, the reindeer, and the urus."

The flint implements of the gravel drift at Ponte Mammolo, and the Ponte Molle near Rome, are witnesses of a very early and rude population in Italy.

Numerous caves in England, in Belgium, in central and southern France, in Italy, in Sicily, in Malta, and elsewhere have yielded almost exactly the same kind of evidence with regard to the existence of men associated with remains of the mammoth, the reindeer, gigantic extinct bear, a large hyæna, and other animals now called cavern animals.

The condition of these dwellers in caves implies a very low and degraded mode of existence. The bones of the reindeer, and other animals, split open for the marrow, and the rude implements in connection with them, testify to this. From the presence of the stone hammers and mortars, it has been suspected that, like some of the savage tribes of Africa, not content with the flesh of the animals which they killed, they pounded up also the bones in mortars, and then sucked out the animal juices contained in them.

Mr. Boyd Dawkins discovered in the Woky hole hyæna den, implements of flint and chert, of the rudest workmanship, associated with bones of the rhinoceros tichorinus, and hyæna spelæa, from which he inferred that man in one of the earliest, if not the earliest stages of his being, dwelt in this cave, as some of the most degraded of our race do at present.

Evidences have been also discovered which lead to a strong suspicion of cannibalism among this earliest race of men.

Dr. Falconer has come to the conclusion (from the human implements and fossil remains of extinct animals discovered by him in the Grotto di Maccagnone in the basin of Palermo) that there is a strong presumptive proof "that the date of man's occupation, in the savage state, of Sicily, went back to a period extremely remote, as compared with the accepted chronology, biblical or profane, when the Mediterranean was bridged over by land connecting Sicily with Africa, as a promontory of that continent."

A grotto has been lately discovered by Professor Capellini, in the island of Palmeria, near Spezzia, where in excavations were found numerous flint and stone implements, the workmanship of the earliest period of the stone age, and the bones of animals mingled with bones of human beings. The condition of the latter bones, Professor Capellini says, denotes that the grotto had been inhabited by anthropophagi, and that the Italians of that epoch were cannibals, like their contemporaries in Belgium, France, and Denmark.

In the opinion of Mr. Boyd Dawkins, it seems probable that the cave of Casa da Mourra in Portugal was inhabited by a race of cannibals. The condition of the human bones found there, indicated that the men to whom they belonged had been eaten for food.

The rude inhabitants of Tierra del Fuego, who feed principally on shell-fish, probably present analogous features to those who lived on the Danish shores in the earliest period, traces of which they have left in the kitchen-middens or shell heaps; and Darwin describes the inhabitants of Tierra del Fuego as living chiefly on shell-fish, and obliged constantly to change their place of residence, but returning at intervals to the same spots, as is evident from the pile of old shells. They are stunted in their growth, their hideous faces bedaubed with white paint, their skins filthy and greasy, their gestures violent and without dignity. Viewing such men, one can hardly make oneself believe they are fellow-creatures, and inhabitants of the same world."

Mr. Tristam adduces proofs of an early rude phase also in Syria. He has discovered in a cave near Beyrout, that the hard limestone of the rock was a mass of bone breccia, with fragments of flint chips mingled in the stalagmite. The bones, he says, are all in fragments, the remains, in all probability, of the feasts of the makers of the rude implements. From the existence of this hard limestone, he adds, we may conclude that when Rameses or his Roman successors constructed their military road, the stone was as compact and crystalline as it is to-day, and many ages must have intervened between the time of the tablets on the rocks, and the days when some rude savage fabricated his weapons on the soft floor of the cavern.

India, too, has yielded her witnesses of the high antiquity of man, and of the degraded condition of the earliest stage of his existence in the rude quartzite implements discovered in the laterite formation at Madras, presenting analogous forms to those of Amiens and Abbeville. They compel a belief that the men who made these implements must have been in similar circumstances, and in a similar condition to the savages who fabricated similar implements on the banks of the Somme and the Ouse, and that they must have occupied the same level of intelligence and skill.

Mr. Page remarks that the occurrence of implements of quartzite in Southern India similar to the flint tools of Western Europe demonstrate the same simple beginnings, and imply a long upward ascent from workers in stone to workers in metal, and thus be it observed, at a period ages before man had found his way westward to the caves and river valleys of France and Belgium.*

America, too, has not been backward in bearing her testimony to the antiquity of the human race, and of its earliest barbarous phase. Dr. Koch gives an account of a mastodon found in Gasconade county, Missouri, which had apparently been stoned to death by the Indians, and then partially consumed by fire.

Dr. Lund has discovered in certain limestone caverns in the Brazils, closely resembling the ossiferous caves of Europe, relics of human skeletons which, from their condition, and the circumstances in which

* "Man, where, whence, and whither," p. 139.

they were discovered, he was led to conclude belonged to a tribe coeval with some of the extinct mammalia.

Lastly, we are told that, before the arrival of the children of the sun, Peru was divided among several, wandering and fixed, rude and ferocious, races, ignorant of all industry and culture, more resembling brutes than the human race.

Of the higher phases in the ascending scale, we find frequent evidence among different nations.

Egypt, being the earliest civilized nation, and where civilization earliest reached its height, any traces of its early phases must be very remote. Evidences of a rude early stage have been lately discovered on the elevated plateau which divides the celebrated valley of Biban el Molouk from the escarpments, which overlook the Pharaonic edifices of Deir-el-Bahari, where has been ascertained the presence of a number of wrought flints, lying on the ground. These wrought flints, which are of the well known type designated arrow-heads, lance-heads, scrapers, &c., evidently belong to a pre-historic age, as they exactly resemble those known in England under the denomination of Neolithic. In Herodotus we find a record of a pastoral stage in Egypt, who relates that the Egyptians commonly called the pyramids after Philition, a shep-

herd who had fed his flocks about the place at a period
before they were built.* This tradition of a shepherd
grazing his flocks where the pyramids now stand,
must therefore point to a very remote period, when
we consider that the pyramids themselves are over
4000 years old.

An agricultural phase was developed at an early
period in Egypt. Sir Gardner Wilkinson tells us
that the Egyptians were thought to have had the
best opportunities of obtaining an accurate knowledge
on all subjects connected with husbandry, and as
Diodorus observes, " being from infancy brought up
to agricultural pursuits, they far excelled the husband-
men of other countries, and had become acquainted
with the capabilities of the land, the mode of irriga-
tion, the exact season for sowing and reaping, as well
as all the most useful secrets connected with harvest,
which they had derived from their ancestors, and had
improved by their own experience." Paintings on
the tomb of Beni-Hassan, representing all the processes of agriculture, date from the reign of Osirtasen I.,
2000 years B.C.

In Western Asia we have also evidences tending
to similar conclusions with regard to a sequence of
phases. Of the hunting phase we have a traditional

* "Herodotus," book ii. 128.

record in Nimrod, who was a mighty hunter. Among the early Chaldeans, Nergal was the god of war and the chase, and Mr. Rawlinson tells that the wild boar was eaten by the primitive people of that country.

The age of Abraham exhibits a pastoral phase. Like an Arab sheikh, " Abraham was rich in cattle," " and Lot also, which went with Abraham, had flocks and herds and tents." The Chaldeans, from whom Abraham derived his origin, were essentially a pastoral people.

> " Chaldean shepherds, ranging trackless fields
> Beneath the concave of unclouded skies,
> Spread like a sea."
> WORDSWORTH.

Professor Rawlinson thus notices the agricultural phase : " A large, probably the largest, portion of the people must have been engaged in the occupations of agriculture. Babylonia was before all things a grain producing country, noted for a fertility unexampled elsewhere, and to moderns almost incredible. The soil was a deep and rich alluvium ; and was cultivated with the utmost care. It grew chiefly wheat, barley, millet, and sesame, which flourished with wonderful luxuriance."

According to Dodwell, the earliest inhabitants of

Greece, the Dryopes, Caucones, Aones, Leleges, were uncultivated savages, who made a casual and temporary residence wherever they were attracted by the fertility of the soil, the abundance of water, or by considerations of weal, security, and protection. These were evidently the Greeks in their early hunting phase, of which Mr. Finlay has discovered such important proofs in the number of obsidian arrow heads found everywhere in the country. It is admitted by all writers, Sir John Stoddart observes, that the original inhabitants of Greece were mere savages, feeding on acorns, living in caves, and clothing themselves in skins of beasts. Of a pastoral stage we have a record in Arcadia, while the Pelasgi, who were an agricultural people, and had attained some skill in metallurgy, were the Greeks in an agricultural phase.

Italy affords evidence of a similar sequence of phases, for we have good grounds for believing that the Osci were the early inhabitants in a rude, hunting stage, while we know with historical certainty that the Siculi were a pastoral people, and that the Pelasgi were in the agricultural phase. Of this we have certain evidence, as the Latin words such as *bos*, *aratrum*, and others connected with agriculture, are known to be of Pelasgic origin.

The earliest known inhabitants of Italy are called by Cato, and other writers, aborigines, a term which, as Micali observes, must not be understood to signify a distinct race, native or foreign, but to apply as a generic title to the tribes of Italy, who were in that rude and barbarous state of society, which constitutes the first steps of human civilization.

In Ireland we find an analogy to this giving the names of distinct peoples to the different phases of civilization of the same people. The so-called three races, the Milesians, the Firbolgians, and the Tuath de Danaans were evidently the primitive indigenous inhabitants in their different phases of civilization. The Milesians, the early Irish, in the hunting phase; the Firbolgians, in the pastoral; and the Tuath de Danaans in the agricultural. We have some evidence in favour of this view. Smith, in his history of Cork, says that Milvyr, in the old Irish and British tongue, signifies an inhabitant of the woods, and from hence they call huntsmen, "Milgi;" and Baxter thinks that the derivation probably of the Irish race, called Miledgh or Milesian, was from this word Milgi, *i.e.* hunters. Sir W. Wilde characterizes the Firbolgians as a simple pastoral people, who professed little knowledge of art, science, and war, and the Tuath de Danaans as promoters of agriculture and metal workers. Sir

W. Wilde gives also an interesting fact, which would tend to show that in reality there was, in ancient times, but one race in Ireland. His words are, "It is a fact curious, but generally overlooked by Irish historians, who bring hither colonies of different nations, that there are but the remains of *one* language, known in manuscript or spoken amongst us."

In England we meet traces of the same phases in the ascending scale. Long before the arrival of the Romans, the Britons had attained but a low degree of civilization, they lived principally by the chase, and had no habitations better than rude wigwams. In the time of Cæsar, they were in a pastoral stage. From Cæsar's description we learn they did not cultivate the earth, but lived on flesh or milk. The greater part of the island was given up to pasture. Agriculture is said to have been introduced by the Belgæ, later settlers.

We need not enter at length on the evidence of a similar upward progress in France, in describing its rude hunting phase in the epoch of the reindeer, its pastoral phase, and its agricultural phase among the Celts.

In Switzerland we trace the same sequence. The discovery near Friedrickshafen, on the lake of Constance, of a number of flint knives and other implements of silex, in conjunction with the bones of the reindeer, of bears of large size, affords evidence of an early race who lived by the chase. The pastoral and agricultural phases we trace in the lake dwellings of Mooseedorf and Wauwyl, and of Morges and Nidau, from the presence of the remains of sheep, cows, horses, and other animals indicative of a pastoral life in the former two, and from the evidences of tillage in the presence of cereals, and the great number of corn-crushers in those of Morges and Nidau. In the opinion of Mr. Rochet and Professor Rutimeyer, the inhabitants of all these lake-dwellings were the same indigenous population (autocthones) in their different stages of gradual improvement.

In the presence of the numberless flint arrow-heads and spear-heads, found in so many parts of Denmark, we have unquestionable proofs of the existence of a hunting phase amongst the people of that country. Hunting and fishing, as Worsaae says, formed their chief sources of subsistence. For catching fish in rivers, and in the sea, they used hooks, harpoons, and lances of flint, and they possessed boats formed of stems of trees which had been hollowed out for the purpose. When hunting they were armed not only with bows and arrows, but also with lances and hunting knives, the more easily to slay the large animals, whose skins served for garments. Passing through the intermediate pastoral stage, agriculture commenced. Bronze tools gradually supplanted the implements of stone. The forests in the interior of the country were cleared by degrees in proportion as agriculture was more widely extended, and the population increased.

Both Cæsar and Tacitus describe the Germans in their earliest phase as devoted to hunting and war. Like the American savages of the same phase, they hunted during a few months of the year, and then gave up all their time to the sports of the chase. The rest of the year was loitered away in sleep and wine.

Tacitus notices their pastoral phase in the following words: "The pride of the German consists in the number of his flocks and herds; they are his only riches, and in them he places his chief delight."

Of their initial steps in agriculture, he observes, "In cultivating the soil, they do not settle on one spot, but shift from place to place. The state or community takes possession of a certain tract proportioned to its number of hands, allotments are afterwards made to individuals according to their rank and dignity. In so extensive a country, where there is no want of land, the partition is easily made. The ground tilled in one year, lies fallow the next, and a sufficient quantity always remains, the labour of the people being by no means adequate to the extent or goodness of the soil."

The aborigines of India are said to have been foresters and mountaineers, leading a wild and lawless life. This must have been at a very remote period, for there is abundance of proof that an advanced state of civilization prevailed previous to the time of the Greek notices of India. Their mode of life must have been somewhat like that of the hill tribes of the extreme south of the Peninsula at the present day, who have only very primitive weapons, and subsist on jungle produce, berries, wild honey, and such like.

Some of the archaic Sanscrit words indicate, by their hoary antiquity, the pastoral employment and character of this people at a very remote date; the special term, for example (the "pasu," of the old Sanscrit or Zend), which signified "private" property among that ancient race, and which we now use under the English modifications, "peculiar," and "pecuniary," primarily meant "flocks," or possession of flocks; the Sanscrit word for protector, and ultimately for the king himself, "go-pa" is the old word for cowherd, and consecutively for chief herdsman, while the endearing name of "daughter" (the *duhitar* of the Sanscrit) is derived from a verb which shows the original signification of the appellation to have been the "milker" of cows. According to Professor Muller, all the Sanscrit words, composed with "go," cattle, prove that the people who formed them must have led a half nomadic and pastoral life.

At a later period we have a record of an agricultural phase. The Aryans, the so-called progenitors of the Hindoos, are said to have been an agricultural people, deriving their name from the root "ar," to plough. At the present day the Hindoo pursues identically the same rude system of agriculture as was followed by his ancestors in the earliest ages.

Herodotus describes the Scythians in their different phases. As a rude and barbarous people; as a hunting people, who employed much of their time in the chase, and who were famous for their management of the bow; as a pastoral people who did not cultivate the ground, but led a pastoral life. Gibbon remarks, "In every age, the immense plains of Scythia or Tartary have been inhabited by vagrant tribes of hunters and shepherds, whose indolence refuses to cultivate the earth, and whose restless spirit disdains the confinement of a sedentary life."

In America we find the hunting phase widely

prevailing from the north to the south. The savage tribes of America were essentially a hunting people.

The absence of a pastoral stage in America has been remarked. If however we find no traces of a strictly pastoral life in the new world, there are at least evidences of an intermediate phase, a transitional stage, a period of stationary existence, a cessation of the wild life of the chase, which prepared a people of huntsmen for the agricultural phase.

The following is a description of the American Indians in a more advanced stage, by one who carefully studied them. "The red men whom our fathers met on the Atlantic seaboard, were of chivalric, though savage race; who showed noble qualities; who were brave, hospitable, magnanimous. They kept their plighted faith, they respected the chastity of women. They made a great advance from the savage state, for they ceased to live by the chase only; they had learnt some part of the herdsman's duty, and the husbandman's craft."

Prescott also bears testimony to a more advanced stage, one beyond the savage hunting phase. He says, "Husbandry to a very limited extent, indeed, was practised by most of the rude tribes of North America. Wherever a natural opening in the forest or a rich strip of *interval* met their eyes, or a green slope was formed along the rivers, they planted it with beans and Indian corn. The cultivation was slovenly in the extreme, and could not secure the improvident natives from the frequent recurrence of desolating famines. Still that they tilled the soil at all was a peculiarity which honourably distinguished them from other tribes of hunters, and raised them *one* degree higher in the scale of civilization."

Sir John Lubbock also shows that the tribes who raised the more southern enclosures, appear to have been more civilized than those of the north, since they were agricultural in their habits, lived in considerable towns, and had a systematized religion, so that, in fact, they must have occupied a *position intermediate*, as well economically, as geographically, between the powerful monarchies of Central America, and the hunting tribes of the north.*

This affords an important proof of self-development, and of spontaneous and independent civilization in America, for, as Sir John Lubbock observes,

* Mr. Fergusson seems, however, inclined to think that the mound-builders were a pastoral people. He says, "Rude Stone Monuments," p. 517: "The red men who occupied North America have never risen beyond the condition of hunters, and have no settled place of abode, and possess no works of art. The mound-builders, on the contrary, were a settled people, certainly pastoral, probably to some extent even agricultural."

"American agriculture resulted from the gradual development of American semi-civilization." This is proved by the fact that the grains of the old world were entirely absent, and that American agriculture was founded on the maize, an American plant.

The only two nations in America, who emerged from this phase, and advanced to a higher civilization, were the Mexicans and Peruvians. In these two nations, we have a further proof of two races, emerging independently and spontaneously from a state of barbarism, and attaining a high point in the scale of civilization. They thus present the important evidence of self-developed civilization.

The Mexicans after a series of wanderings, shifting their quarters to different parts, enduring all the casualties and hardships of a migratory life, in which they must have passed through the many phases of a people struggling to emerge from a state of barbarism, and to attain a higher stage, settled at last on the borders of the Lake of Tezcuco, where they advanced to a comparatively high state of civilization. The legend of Quetzalcoatl, a divinity who, during his residence on earth, instructed the nations in the use of metals, in agriculture, and in the arts of governing, is a record of the development of the agricultural phase.

With regard to the earlier phase in Peru, Mr.

Prescott tells us, that the time was, when the ancient races were plunged in deplorable barbarism, when they worshipped nearly every object in nature indiscriminately; made war their pastime, and feasted on the flesh of the slaughtered captives. Like other savages in the same phase, they lived on the wild game of the forest and the mountain, which they hunted down.

The flocks of Llama (the Peruvian sheep), wandering with their shepherds over the broad wastes on the crests of the Sierra, bears testimony to the existence of a pastoral stage among the early inhabitants of Peru. The number of the flocks at a later period, we are told, was immense; they were scattered over the different provinces, under the care of experienced shepherds, who conducted them to different pastures, according to the change of season. In the employment of domestic animals the Peruvians were distinguished from the other races of the new world.

The fiction of Manco Capac teaching agriculture, is only the mythical account of the agricultural phase, which reached a high state of perfection under the Incas. These civilizers, such as Quetzalcoatl, Manco Capac, and other analogous mythic personages in other countries, are only the personifications of a step in the progress of civilization.

This closes our chapter on the earliest phases of man, and we think sufficient evidence has been adduced to prove the progressive development of man from a rude and barbarous stage, through successive phases, up to a higher state of civilization, and that an invariable law of upward progress is followed among all higher races. Further, this progressive development presents a strong presumption in favour of the belief in the existence of an invariable sequence in all things, that they pass through certain fixed phases and stages of development in the ascending scale from a lower to a higher.

ON THE DEGRADED PHASE.

An objection has been made to the view, that races in a savage and barbarous phase are in their original state; that they are in reality in a degraded and degenerate stage, having previously been civilized.

On carefully examining these phases, we shall find that they can be easily distinguished, as they are distinct, and belong to different epochs of civilization.

It is unquestionable that many races and nations have retrograded and relapsed into barbarism, and, in some instances, have returned to their primitive savage state.

The degeneration of race is the necessary result of the law of the cycle of development; all things run through their cyclical course. They have their rise, maturity, decline, and decay; the races which are now degenerated and degraded had once attained the height of civilization, passing through all the successive phases of civilization in the ascending scale.

On reaching the culminating point of civilization, it is the destiny of all nations and races to decline, decay, and return to their original barbarous state. Nations, like individuals in their extreme old age, return to the early condition of childhood. The savage and barbarous stage is the first phase, the degraded, the last phase in the cycle of development of nations and races.

The races in the degraded phase can be easily distinguished from the races in their state of barbarism. We know the history of the degenerate races, we have evidences of their having once attained a state of civilization; we have proofs of it in the remains of the architecture, sculpture, of these races, and in their historical records.

One of the most important examples of a degenerate race, are the Fellahs of Egypt. This degraded, ignorant, filthy class of Mohammedan Fellahs, are the most direct descendants of the ancient Egyptian people, who conquered Ethiopia, and overran Asia, and whose learning was a light even to Grecian philosophers; but we know, with every certainty, that the Egyptians being a self-developed people, arose from a barbarous state, and gradually passing through successive phases, reached the highest civilization, and fulfilling the laws of their cycle of development, they declined, decayed, and ultimately became the degenerate race we now see in the Fellahs.

The modern Peruvians and Mexicans are thus in a similar degraded phase. The present degraded Aztecs and Peruvians, are the same people whom the Spaniards found, only some three hundred years ago, dwelling in splendid palaces, and worshipping their unknown gods in golden temples, through the medium of a sacred tongue.

With regard to races in their original barbarous and savage state, and which, as yet, have never made an onward step towards a higher phase, we have indubitable evidence. The Australians, the Andaman Islanders, the Veddahs, the Patagonians, the Fuegians, and many other races which travellers frequently mention, are in that stage; and further, we have the strongest presumption, amounting to certainty, that the earliest inhabitants of England, France, Denmark, indeed of all Europe, and also of India, were once in a similar state.

ON THE SEQUENCE OF FLINT, STONE, COPPER, AND BRONZE IMPLEMENTS IN ALL COUNTRIES.

My object in this chapter is to bring briefly and more prominently into notice the sequence of flint, stone, and bronze implements in nearly all countries, during their pre-historic ages, by describing, and by giving illustrative examples of those implements, which form a complete sequence from the earliest rude handiwork of man, up to the more elaborately worked and finished specimens of stone and bronze. These examples show the various stages in the progress of the implements, as well as the improvement in the art of their fabrication. They exhibit forms which are determined by a process of development, that is to say, by gradual modifications of rude and early types. They are witnesses of a gradual development of human ingenuity, as applied to purposes of the chase, of warfare, and of domestic life. As Dr. Wilson observes, "Man was created with a tool-using instinct, and with faculties capable of developing it into all the mechanical triumphs which command such wonder and admiration at the present day, but he was also created with a necessity for such. Half the industrial arts are the result of our being born without clothes, the other half, of our being born without tools."

1ST STAGE.—IMPLEMENTS OF THE GRAVEL DRIFT.

The presence of implements of this type in gravel drifts, which geological evidence assigns to a very remote period, and in conjunction with bones of extinct animals, argue a very remote antiquity for their manufacture, and a very early date for the men who fabricated them. The extreme rudeness of the implements bespeak a corresponding rudeness and barbarous condition of the men who made them, and induce a belief in the inferiority of this primitive race.

These implements were evidently roughly knocked into shape. Those found in the gravel drifts of England and France are always rough; and among the many thousands which have been discovered, not one has been met with which shows a trace of polishing and grinding. They are almost always made of flint. Their forms are also peculiar, some oval,

No. 1.

FLINT IMPLEMENT FROM HOXNE—HALF-SIZE.

chipped up to an edge all round, and from two to eight or nine inches in length. A second type is also oval, but somewhat pointed at one end (Fig. 2)—this type has been styled in France *en amande*. Others again have a more or less heavy butt at one end, and are pointed at the other (Fig. 1)—the workmen in

No. 2.

FLINT IMPLEMENT FROM HOXNE—HALF-SIZE.

the valley of the Somme have named these *langues de chat*. Mr. Evans seems to regard them as having served as spears or lance-heads. He treats as a mere variety of this type, those implements in which the cutting end is rounded off, but not pointed. Some of these were evidently intended to be held in the hand, as the Australians use their rude stone hatchets at the present day.*

No. 3.

STONE IMPLEMENT FROM MADRAS.

They vary greatly in size. They are generally about six inches long, by about three inches broad,

* A friend, Mr. Charles Seymour, tells me he has seen Australians hold their stone hatchets in their hands, and with them cut out boomerangs, etc., adopting a kind of circular blow.

but much longer ones are sometimes met with. One found at St. Acheul, and exhibited at the Paris Exhibition, 1867, was eleven and a half inches long, by about five broad.

Implements of this earliest and rudest type have been discovered in many countries. They have been found not only in the gravel drift of England, France, and Spain, but also in the laterite formation near Madras, in India.

Doubts have been thrown on these implements being of human workmanship, but on carefully examining them, the greatest sceptic must admit they bear unmistakably the indications of having been shaped by the skill of man.

These implements, therefore, have a deep claim on our interest, as they make known to us the earliest productions of the hand of man, as they mark the first step in human industry, and as they show, in the most unequivocal manner, "the length of time which must have elapsed since the first appearance of man in Western Europe."

2ND STAGE.—FLINT FLAKES.

In this stage we have flint flakes of the simplest form, such as were frequently struck off, for the purpose of being used as arrow-heads, lances, rude knives, &c. One side being smooth, and slightly convex, owing to the conchoidal fracture of the flint, the other generally exhibiting two or three faces. The two side ones having a sharp edge. Flint appears, as Sir J. Lubbock observes, "to have been the stone most often used in Europe, and it has had a

No. 4.

FLINT CORE—IRELAND.

No. 5.

FLINT FLAKE—DENMARK.

much more important influence on our civilization than is generally supposed. Savages value it on account of its hardness and mode of fracture. A good sound block can be chipped into almost any form that may be required."

If an ordinary oblong flint nodule be broken

across in the middle, the fracture is conchoidal, or shell-shaped, and if one of the portions of that flint were set on end, the artist could chop off with a

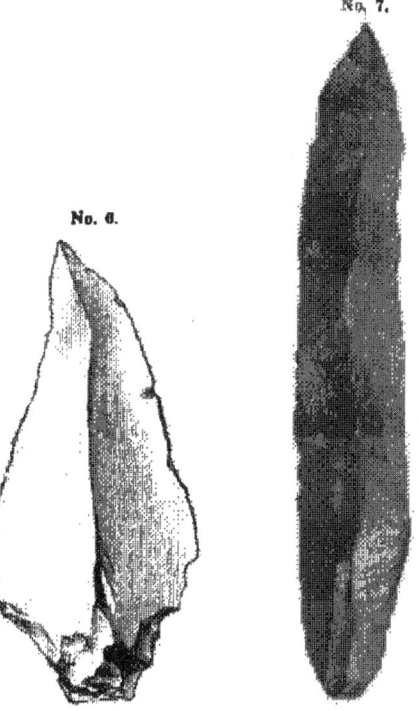

No. 6. ARROW SHAPED FLINT FLAKE—IRELAND.
No. 7. FLINT FLAKE—DENMARK.

hammer, or with a chisel and mallet, a number of fine flakes, running the length of the sides of the mass; more or less thin and long, or broad and thick, according to the natural purity of the flint, and perhaps the dexterity of the worker. Each scale or flake, no matter what its outer shape or outline, will always present the conchoidal fracture. The outside flakes, bearing the usual rough silicate of lime investiture, were generally valueless, and consequently cast aside. In striking off these flakes, the tool used must have been a stone or flint; but of what precise nature we have as yet no definite information. In chipping or scaling a mass of flint, the artist appears to have struck it on the end, and as he passed round the block, striking in the centre of the angle made by the junction of any two chips, the scale must always have presented more or less of an obtusely triangular figure in its section; and owing to the tapering nature of the flint mass, a leaf-like outline, which, from the peculiar fracture or cleavage of all flint, it was curved in the longitudinal direction, and also slightly convex from side to side upon the under surface.* This under surface is invariably smooth, and, to a certain degree, polished; but, from the deficiency of lines upon it, and its invariable curvature, it can easily be distinguished from the smoothing and

* At the base of the flat side of this flake thus struck off, there is always what is called the bulb of percussion, which is a slight bulb-like swelling where it has been struck off by a blow from the flint nodule.

polishing produced by art. The edges of nearly all these flakes are sharp, and generally meet at a point at the extremity, while the butt, or portion to which the tool was applied, is usually chipped and broken, as if it required repeated blows to get it off. Each surface in the convex aspect is smooth, though occasionally presenting the wave-like appearance of broken glass. This was the first attempt at a weapon or tool of stone. The artist, it would appear, chipped off as many scales or flakes as the mass would afford, and then threw aside the core or spud, when it ceased to be any longer useful.* These flint flakes generally vary in size from half an inch to four and a half inches in length, and from three-eighths of an inch to three inches across at the broadest part."†

It is said that flakes are struck off more readily from the flint when fresh from the chalk, and that the edges are much sharper, than when struck off from a flint which has been for some time exposed to, and hardened by, the air.

In the case of obsidian, the flakes were made, not

* In the above examples, the development is marked. No. 5, is a simple flake. No. 6, is a flake chipped at the base. No. 7, is a flake chipped over on one side. These flakes present almost identical forms in any country where the primitive inhabitants could obtain flint or obsidian.

† Sir W. Wilde's "Catalogue of the Royal Irish Academy," p. 7.

by blows, but by strong pressure, as was done by the Mexicans, and as the Esquimaux of the present do with their chert implements. Sir E. Belcher thus describes their mode of operating. "Selecting" he

No. 8.

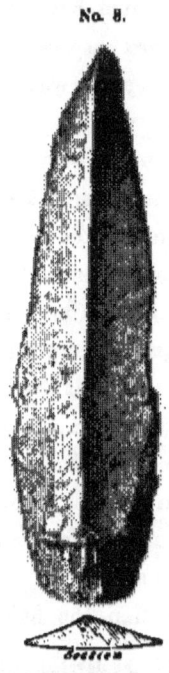

AUSTRALIAN FLAKE.

says, "a log of wood, in which a spoon-shaped cavity was cut, they placed the splinter to be worked over it, and by pressing gently along the margin vertically, first on one side, then the other, as one would set a saw, they splintered off alternate fragments, until the object, thus properly outlined, presented the spear or arrow-head form, with two cutting serrated sides.

To enumerate all the different parts of the world in which flakes, either of flint, obsidian, chert, &c., showing almost identical forms, have been discovered, would fill pages, and would include nearly the entire surface of the globe. The manufacture of these flakes as weapons, from the above substances, seems to have been suggested independently and spontaneously among many races. The presence also of cores,* which have had flakes knocked off from them, in Denmark, England, Ireland, India, Mexico, Greece, &c., show further the independent and indigenous origin of these flint flakes in these countries. Several places have been discovered which may be considered as the manufactories of these flint flakes, where, from the countless numbers met with, they must have been

* (See Fig. 4.) The chert cores found in India, in the bed of the river Indus, in Upper Scinde, are remarkable for the beautiful regularity of their form, showing the facets from which the last flakes dislodged have been struck off, with the bulbs of percussion distinctly marked. The author possesses three of these cores, kindly presented by Major-General Twomlow. The obsidian cores from Mexico also exhibit the same regularity of form. Mr. Finlay tells me that a large number of obsidian cores have been lately discovered in Greece, at Salagora, near Arta.

largely manufactured; the flint used being close at hand. One of the most remarkable of these manufactories is that discovered by Dr. Leveillé, at Pressigny le Grand, in France, about half way between Tours and Poitiers. Here there is an abundance of good flint, of a honey colour, and even though coarse texture. This flint was largely used in ancient times. The fields are covered with nuclei, flakes, &c.; and implements made here, and easily recognizable by the peculiar colour, have been found

No. 9.

FLINT CORE FROM PRESSIGNY. Ten inches long. Demmin's "Weapons of War."

in various parts of France. Another of these manufactories has been lately discovered in Egypt. On the elevated plateau which divides the celebrated valley of Biban-el-Molouk, from the escarpments which overlook the Pharaonic edifices of Deir-el-Bihan, the presence of an enormous quantity of wrought flints, lying on the surface of the ground, to the extent of upwards of a hundred square yards, has been ascertained by Messrs. Hamy and Le Normant. These wrought flints evidently constitute the remains of an ancient manufactory.

3rd stage.

We now approach a more advanced stage in handicraft and design, in which the flint flakes were carefully chipped into shape, apparently by a succession of slight taps, or gentle but well directed blows with some sharp-pointed tool. At first but one side (the ordinary convex one) was chipped, and then, in the more perfect implement, both sides were thus manufactured, long practice leading to their being formed of a symmetrical shape and elegant proportion. The chief object in the careful manufacture of the arrow-head, was that they might fly well. In illustration we shall quote Catlin's description* of the mode in which modern American Indians manufacture their arrow-heads. "Their mode of manufacturing arrow-heads is very simple, and evidently the only mode by which those peculiar shapes, and delicacy of fracture, can possibly be produced; for civilized artizans have tried in various parts of the world, and with the best of tools, without success in copying them.

"Every tribe has its factory, in which their arrow-heads are made, and in those, only certain adepts are

* "Last Rambles among the Indians," p. 187.

able or allowed to make them, for the use of the tribe. Erratic boulders of flint are collected (and sometimes brought an immense distance), and broken with a sort of sledge hammer made of a rounded pebble of horn-stone set in a twisted withe, holding the stone, and forming a handle.

"The flint, at the indiscriminate blows of the sledge, is broken into a hundred pieces, and such flakes selected as, from the angles of their fracture and thickness, will answer as the basis of an arrow-head; and in the hands of the artizan they are shaped into the beautiful forms and proportions which they desire, and which are to be seen in most of our museums.

"The master workman, seated on the ground, lays one of these flakes on the palm of his left hand, holding it firmly down with two or more fingers of the same hand, and with his right hand between the thumb and two fore-fingers, places his chisel (or punch) on the point that is to be broken off; and a co-operator (a striker), sitting in front of him, with a mallet of very hard wood, strikes the chisel (or punch) on the upper end, flaking the flint off on the under side, below each projecting point that is struck. The flint is then turned and chipped in the same manner from the opposite side, and so turned and chipped until the required shape and dimensions are obtained, all the fractures being made on the palm of the hand.

"In selecting a flake for the arrow-head, a sure judgment must be used, or the attempt will fail; a flake with two opposite parallels, or nearly parallel planes, is found, and of the thickness required for the centre of the arrow point. The first chipping reaches near to the centre of these planes, but without quite breaking it away, and each chipping is shorter and shorter, until the shape and the edge of the arrow-head are formed.

"The yielding elasticity of the palm of the hand, enables the chip to come off without breaking the body of the flint, which would be the case, if they were broken on a hard substance. These people have no metallic instruments to work with, and the instrument (punch) which they use, I was told, was a piece of bone; but on examining it, I found it to be a substance much harder, made of the tooth (incisor) of the sperm whale, or sea lion, which are often stranded on the coast of the Pacific. This punch is about six or seven inches in length, and one inch in diameter, with one rounded side, and two plane sides; therefore presenting one acute and two obtuse angles, to suit the points to be broken.

"This operation is very curious, both the holder and the striker singing, and the strokes of the mallet given exactly in time with the music, and with a sharp *rebounding* blow, in which, the Indians tell us, is the great *medicine* (or mystery) of the operation."

The various sizes of these implements may be generally attributed to the nature of the game which the natives hunted. For example, a large spear-head may have been used as a war instrument, or for killing large animals, while the smaller ones—arrow-heads, were used for the destruction of small animals and birds.

Sir William Wilde classes the different shapes of arrow-heads of flint under five varieties, which exhibit a series of development from the rudest form. First is the *triangular* (No. 10), or the simplest form, which frequently had a notch on each side, to receive the string which attached it to the shaft, a variety common at the present day among the American Indians. It was then hollowed out at the base to such an extent that in process of time it assumed the *indented* (No. 11), or second variety of this series. The third is the *stemmed* * arrow-head, having a tang or projection for sticking into the shaft, and the wings on either side of which gradually

* See Plate I., Figures 10, 11, 22.

bend into the "broad arrow" shape. By prolonging the wings until they extended as low as the central stem, the fourth variety was attained, or what may be denominated the true *barbed arrow* (No. 12). The fifth variety is the *leaf shaped* (No. 13), generally very thin, and chipped all over with great care. It is much more simple in shape than any of the fore-

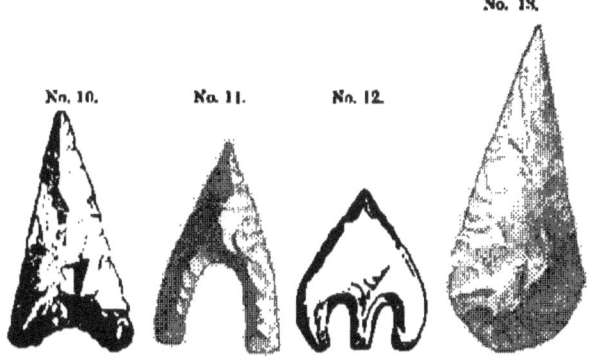

going, but it has been placed at the end of the series, because it leads to the final and more perfect flint manufacture of the weapon-class, that of the spear. The spear-head is thus only a larger and longer development of the arrow-head.* Spear-heads are very variable in size and form. Some of them are scarcely distinguished from large arrow-heads, others

* See Plate I., Nos. 4, 14.

are much larger and longer. Some Danish spear-heads, of most beautiful workmanship, are twelve inches in length.

Some of the Danish arrow-heads, lance-heads, and daggers of flint belonging to this stage, exhibit a beauty and delicacy of finish which are marvellous, and far beyond the skill of workmen of the present day.

The Japanese and Peruvian arrow-heads of quartzite are also of exquisite workmanship, and exhibit identical forms to those of Europe.

The Mexican arrow-heads of obsidian are remarkable for their wonderful finish, far exceeding that of the chipped flints of Scandinavia. Mr. Tylor challenges an ingenious artist in England, who makes arrow-heads for the benefit of English antiquaries, to imitate their ribbed, obsidian spear-heads.

Arrow-heads, spear-heads carefully chipped, belonging to this more advanced stage, of flint, agate, obsidian, quartzite, and of other substances, of almost identical shape and form, and for similar purposes, have been discovered nearly all over the world. Examples of these which have been used by the most ancient races in the earliest times, occur not only in Egypt, Palestine, Arabia, Chaldæa, Italy, Greece, England, Ireland, Denmark, France, and Switzerland, but also in India, Japan, Peru, Mexico, North and South

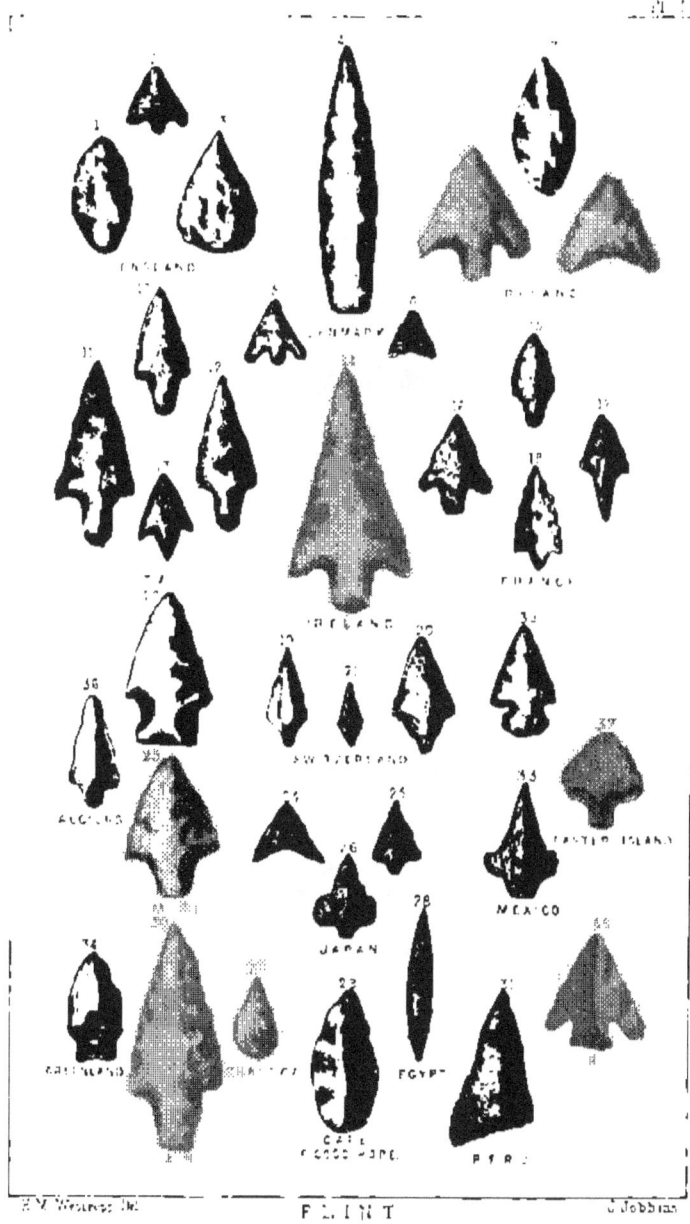

America, and North and South Africa.* Similar weapons are also met with among all the savage tribes of the present day.

DANISH AXE GROUND AT THE EDGE.

DANISH FLINT HATCHET. From Demmin's " Weapons of War."

* Plate L shows the great similarity of arrow-heads, whether of flint, obsidian, or quartzite, in countries the most widely apart. In this plate are two arrow-heads which look so exactly alike that they might have been made by the same hand and on the same day. Yet one comes from Scandinavia, and is at least two thousand years old, the other from Tierra del Fuego, and was manufactured not more than twenty years ago.

stated that they vary in length from twenty two inches to very little more than one inch in length, some idea may be formed of the range through which this series of implements extended.*

The celt was the principal tool and weapon, serving the purpose of chisel, punch, wedge, plane, hatchet, and battle-axe among the early Celtic inhabitants of Ireland.

These stone implements were evidently used for handicraft purposes, for cutting and splitting timber, in building houses, for cutting down trees, and on some occasions as weapons.

For the most part, they were fixed in wooden handles. We give illustrations of the modes of hafting stone-hatchets among the Irish and Swiss (Figs. 17, 18), which will give some idea of the various modes better than any description.

Some were evidently held in the hand, as by the Australians of the present day, who thus hold their stone hatchets when cutting notches in trees, when ascending them, and when shaping out their boomerangs.

The distinctions are so marked between the dif-

---

* Mr. Finlay has kindly sent me from Greece the smallest stone celt I have ever seen, it is exactly one inch long, and one and one-eighth in breadth.

ferent stages of the flint and stone age, that they may be divided into three, corresponding with the phases of civilization visible in man.

1st. The flint implements of the gravel drift, and of the cave period, evidently used by man in his lowest and most barbarous grade.

2. The flint implements (the flint flakes, and the chipped flints) found on the surface in England, Ireland, Denmark, and other countries, which belonged to a people who lived by the chase.

3. Ground and polished stone implements which mark a more advanced stage, and which are found associated with traces of a pastoral age.

The chipped flint implements and the polished and ground implements were evidently made for distinct purposes. The chipped flints were obviously fabricated for the purpose of the chase, for killing game of all kinds, and also for warfare; while the ground implements were for handicraft purposes, for cutting down trees, hollowing out canoes, splitting timber, &c. The first were weapons, the latter tools.

The following terms may therefore be used to distinguish the three different stages. The first or Palæolithic, the second or Mesolithic, and the third or Neolithic.

Every nation, even those most anciently civilized, has had its stone age. Stone celts, as Mr. Franks observes,* have been discovered nearly all over the world, most districts of Europe, and also Asia Minor, Egypt, Assyria, India, China, Java, and Japan. have furnished specimens, as have likewise North and South America, North and South Africa, the West Indies, New Caledonia, New Zealand, and Australia. In some of the latter countries they are still in use. The same general type pervades all those countries, though, with some practice, an archæologist will generally be able to determine the locality from which a specimen has been derived, guided by minute differences in form and material. For instance, Irish celts are generally unsymmetrical, and not as highly polished as English specimens, and moreover they are rarely made of flint, the common material for such implements in the south of England. Those from Scandinavia, though made of flint, are of a more opaque kind, and squarer edges, and more uniform thickness than those found in the British Isles.

The material used by the rude and primitive races for their implements, almost always depended on the stone found nearest at hand for that purpose, the hardest and toughest stones being generally selected. The

* "Horæ Feralæ," p. 134.

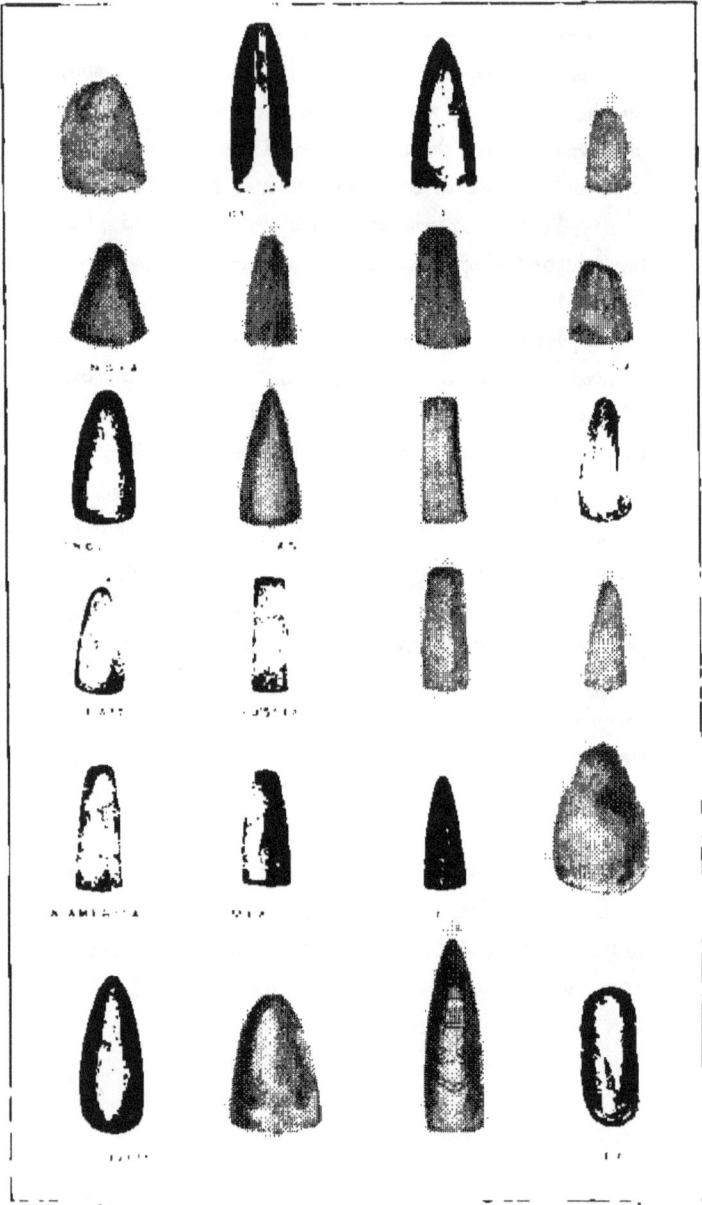

early rude inhabitants of Denmark, Sweden, England, Ireland, and France, generally used flint, and at a later period, green stone (Diorite), serpentine and aphanite.

In regard to the material of Irish celts, Sir W. Wilde remarks: "In material the stone celts afford examples of nearly every description of rock found in Ireland suited for the purpose, by its hardness, toughness, absence of brittleness, and susceptibility of polish; from the hard, sharp silex, the metallic basalt, the highly-polished porphyry, the splintery felstone, the rare syenite, and the compact green stone, to the smooth clay slate or shale, the brittle sandstone grit, the soft whetstone, or even the micaceous schist, with all their different varieties and combinations."

In the Swiss lake dwellings, the implements discovered, were made of materials found in their neighbourhood. At Wangen the rolled stones of the neighbourhood, originally derived from the Rhætian Alps, formed the material of the greater portion of the implements. At Mooseedorf the material appears to have come from the Swiss Jura (chalk), some from the Alps. At Nussdorf, they were made of the rolled stones found in the lake close by. Some also are made of nephrite.*

* The presence of implements of jade in Switzerland has given

Mr. Finlay tells us that many of the implements found in Greece were evidently worked out of the rolled pebbles found in different parts of the country, which were selected from experience of the toughness that was combined with their hardness, and from their natural form requiring the least possible labour to give them the desired shape. Red jaspery, iron clay, and brown argillaceous iron stone are found as rough pebbles in the glens of Eubœa, and celts fashioned from them are not uncommon in the island.

The American Indians used the red stone of the prairies for their arrow-heads.

---

rise to some wild theories of communication with the east, upon which M. Desors makes the following sensible remarks. "We cannot share the opinion which attributes extensive commercial relations to the tribes of the age of stone. In support of this opinion are cited the hatchets of nephrite, of which numbers are found at Concise and other stations of that epoch; and as this stone now comes to us from the East, it has been inferred that the tribes of the remote period in question trafficked with Asia. But it should be remembered that the greater part of the hatchets which are assumed to be nephrite, may very well be only varieties of indigenous rocks, proceeding from siliceous veins in the serpentine, and whose depository might be found, according to M. de Mortillet, in the higher Maurienne. It seems to us very difficult to admit that so distant a commerce should have been restricted to the exchange of certain stones which, after all, are not very superior to common silex, while the East might have furnished objects of far greater utility, particularly metals."—*Desor's Palafittes, Smithsonian Report*, p. 368.

Quartzite was the material generally adopted by the Japanese and the Peruvians.

Arrow-heads of crystal have been found in Switzerland, crystal being abundant there. Lance-heads of crystal have been also found at Guayaquil, in South America.

In Mexico and Tenerife, obsidian has been found in great quantities. Its presence has suggested its use for similar purposes. The Mexicans used obsidian for their arrow-heads. It was also employed for knives, razors, &c. In like manner the Guanches (the ancient inhabitants of Tenerife) fixed splinters of that mineral to the end of their lances. In both countries this variety of lava was employed as an object of ornament.

Among the natives of New Zealand, jade, being found in that island, was largely used for their *meris*, hatchets, and other implements, and ornaments. Obsidian, jade, and Lydian stone are, Humboldt remarks, three minerals, which nations, ignorant of the use of copper or iron, have, in all ages, employed for making keen-edged weapons.

We must here remark an error, which often leads to confusion, in the assignment of stone implements to a certain fixed period. It is generally assumed that the stone age has been synchronous in all countries, and among all tribes; whereas, as Mr. Franks observes, in each country, and even in each tribe, the change from stone to metal may have taken place at very different times. It is important, he adds, to remember this, as it may account sometimes for apparent anomalies, such as the discovery together of implements of the two materials, due, perhaps, to some encounter between tribes differently armed.

The use of stone implements will be always according to the stage of civilization of the nation or country in which they are found, and not at any fixed or definite period of time. Their presence is thus not always an evidence of high antiquity, but of a rude and barbarous state, for stone hatchets are found in common use at the present day among the South Sea islanders. Some tribes of Indians have been recently met with, near the sources of the Purus river, in South America, still using their primitive stone hatchets. In New Zealand, and Australia also, they are still in use. The remoteness of the stone age of any country must therefore be inferred from the relative antiquity of the country in which they are found. Thus the flint and stone implements found in Egypt, or India, will belong to a remoter period than those found in Denmark, England, or France, while the latter will be witnesses of an earlier age than those which are met with in New Zealand and Australia.

6TH STAGE.

Between the stone and bronze ages, there was an intermediate or transitional stage, in which native copper was used for implements, and was hammered cold into shape. Copper being one of the most abundant of metals, its frequent occurrence in its native state, its possessing great malleability, and consequently its readily taking the form desired, makes it probable that the presence of this metal suggested its use for the same purposes, for which stone had been hitherto employed. Native copper was thus rather used as a stone than a metal; advantage being taken of its extreme malleability, it was hammered into form without the assistance of heat. Implements of native copper, hammered into shape, are thus found as the earliest applications of the metal.

Of this stage we have certain evidence in North America. Such implements marking the passage from stone to bronze have been largely used by the race known as the mound builders. Copper occurs frequently in the tumuli raised by them, wrought and unwrought. "All the copper found in the mounds appeared to have been worked in a cold state; and although the axes and other instruments appear to be harder than the copper of commerce, they have been found upon analysis to be destitute of alloy. The superior hardness which they possess over the unworked metal, is doubtless due to the *hammering* to which they have been subjected."—*Squier's Antiquities of New York.*

These mound builders do not seem, as Mr. Tylor observes, to have understood the art of melting copper, or even of forging it hot, but to have treated it as a kind of malleable stone, which they got in pieces out of the ground, or knocked off from the great natural blocks, and hammered into knives, chisels, axes, and ornaments. Professor Dana observes further, that they may in one sense to have been in an age of stone, since they used the copper not as metal, but as a stone.

Evidence of the use of copper in its native state we also find in Ireland. In my collection is a rude hatchet of pure copper, hammered into shape. Examples are, however, exceedingly rare, as the hatchets of pure copper were doubtless all melted down and worked into bronze.

Copper implements were formed on the model of the stone ones. As Sir J. Lubbock observes, "It is interesting to observe that the copper arrow or spear-heads resemble the American type of stone arrow-heads." Thus showing how strictly the sequence is followed in the series of flint, stone, copper, and bronze implements.

The next step in this transitional stage was when

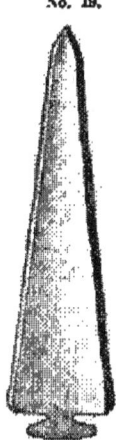
No. 19.

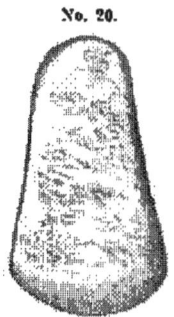
No. 20.

AMERICAN COPPER ARROW-HEAD, HAMMERED.   COPPER CELT CAST—IRELAND.

the copper was melted and moulded into the shape of the implement; an initial stage in metallurgy.

In this progressive step we still find the celt, made of pure copper, melted and moulded into form, keeping the shape of the stone implement. As Sir W. Wilde observes, " The metal celt is but the stone implement reproduced in another form; and having once obtained a better material, the people who acquired this knowledge repeated the form they were best acquainted with, but economised the metal, and lessened the bulk, by flattening the sides." In proof of this repetition in metal of the ancient form of the stone celt, may be adduced the fact of a copper celt of the precise outline, both in shape and thickness, of one of our ordinary stone implements having been found in an Etruscan tomb, and now preserved in the museum in Berlin. In Ireland, also, copper celts occur not unfrequently, having a great similarity to their stone predecessors of the rudest description.

The use of copper for the earliest metal implements is proved by the discovery of implements of that metal, in its pure state, in many countries. A large battleaxe of pure copper was found in Ratho bog, near Edinburgh. Sir W. Wilde, in his "Catalogue of the Royal Irish Academy," says, that upon careful examination, it has been found that thirty of the rudest, and apparently the very oldest celts, are of red, almost unalloyed, copper. Axes of copper, according to Professor Nilsson, are occasionally found in Scania. They have been also found in Switzerland. The one found at Sipplingen is thus described by Dr. Keller: "One single celt was met with of copper,

of very simple form, like that of the stone celts."
Dr. Keller mentions another found at Meurach.
Axes of copper have been also discovered in Italy
(Peschiera), and in Hungary.

They occur also in Greece. Mr. Finlay notices a
small axe of pure copper found in Eubœa, which, as
he justly observes, appears to belong to the transition period, when the use of metal was discovered,
but the form of the stone celt retained.

In Asia numerous implements and weapons of
copper have been discovered in a particular class of
graves; and in some of the old and long abandoned
mines in that country, workman's tools have been
discovered, made of copper, and of very remote
antiquity.

Chisels and tools of pure copper have been also
discovered in Egypt. The copper mines of Wadi
Maghara, in the peninsula of Sinai, were worked
more than three thousand years before our era, by a
colony of labourers from Egypt.

We find evidence of this intermediate stage also in
Mexico and Peru. Prescott tells us that the arrows
and spears of the Peruvians were tipped with copper,
and that the tools used were mostly of that metal.
Mr. Squier, in his history of New York, gives a
sketch of an ancient spear-head of copper found in

a Peruvian *huaca* or tumulus, near Lima. The Spaniards, we are told, mistook the bright copper axes of the Mexicans for gold.

We must add a remark that the copper period, or age of unalloyed metals, appears to have been of a very brief and transitory character in Europe.

7TH STAGE.

We now pass into a more advanced stage of civilization, into what is termed essentially the bronze age.

Finding by experience that an admixture of tin, or an alloy of that metal in certain proportions was necessary to harden the copper, and make it more and more fusible, bronze, or copper, with an alloy of tin, came into general use for implements and weapons among the men of the pre-historic age. On the discovery of the increase of hardness acquired by copper on its admixture with tin, the pure copper implements were doubtless returned to the melting-pot, and reproduced in the more perfect and useful condition of the bronze alloy.

The adoption of bronze could not have been either sudden or universal. The transition from the first rude instrument of flint or stone to the more valuable metal, must have been very gradual, and possibly extended over centuries.

The line of demarcation, however, between the stone and bronze ages was not divided and marked; they frequently overlap and intermingle. In some countries flint and stone implements were retained far into the bronze age.

Human nature, as it has been said, is too conservative to allow an old contrivance to be readily vanquished by a new invention. Bows and arrows were in vogue long after the discovery of gunpowder, and so stone and bronze implements were in use during the age of iron. And as we do not know when these transitional stages of human progress began, so neither can we say when they respectively terminated. In fact, there are savage tribes, such as the Andaman islanders, who are still in the stone age. There is, however, every certainty now that these progressive stages were passed through in almost every country, which exhibited progress and development, but at what time and at what age is uncertain.

In the bronze arrow-heads and spear-heads of this age, the sequence of development is strictly carried out. The earliest forms are copies of the flint arrowhead; thence rising progressively in various transitional forms, until they culminate in the spear-heads of exquisite shape and proportions. They vary in length, from an inch to two feet and a half. Bronze arrow-heads, though occasionally found in Ireland, are almost unknown in England; in Germany they are more plentiful; but the East seems to have been the part of the world in which they were principally used. They are not very common in northern Europe, as Sir J. Lubbock remarks, probably because flint was so much cheaper, and almost as effective.

Arrow-heads with small tangs, in imitation of the flint-stemmed arrow-head, are occasionally found, as well as others, with sockets. Flat spear-heads of bronze, obvious copies of the flint leaf-shaped spear-heads, occur in many countries. Mr. Franks divides those with sockets into two principal classes, viz., those with rivet holes and those without. Where there are no rivet holes we frequently find loops, sometimes placed close to the blade, and forming part of it, sometimes near the lower end of the sockets. These side loops seem to be peculiar to the British Isles, and are rather more common in Ireland than in England.

The swords of the bronze age assume more or less a leaf-like shape, and are evidently further developments of the flint daggers of the stone age. A com-

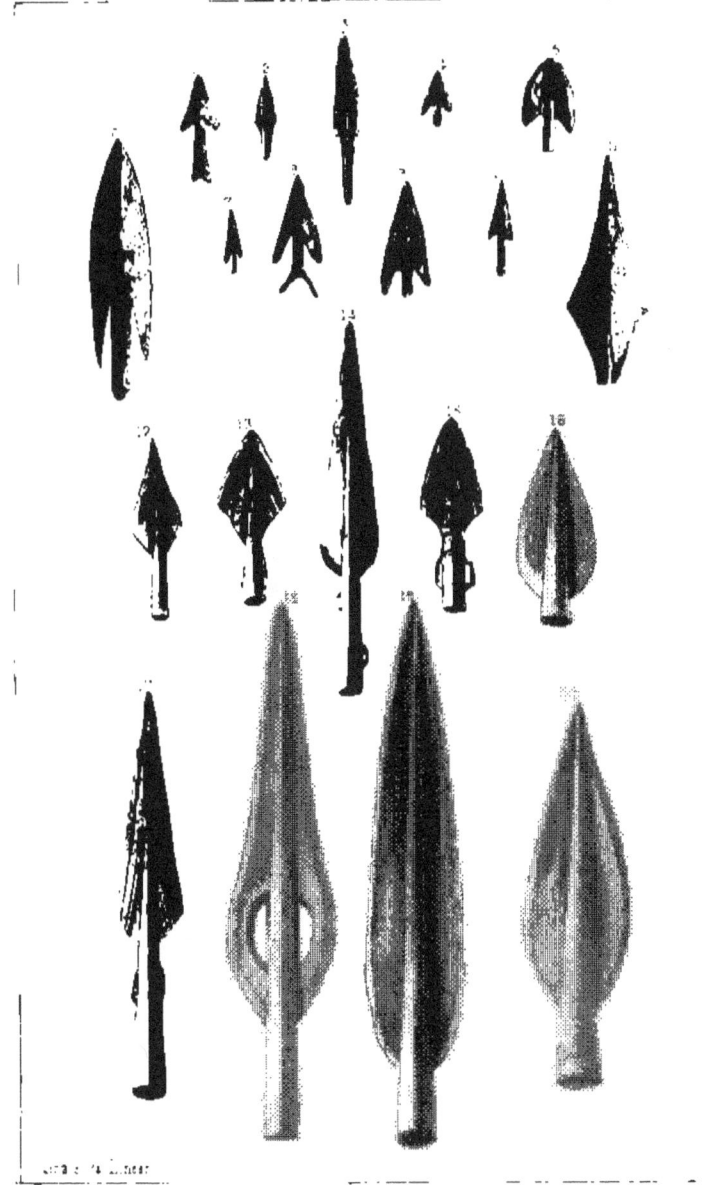

AND BRONZE IMPLEMENTS. 79

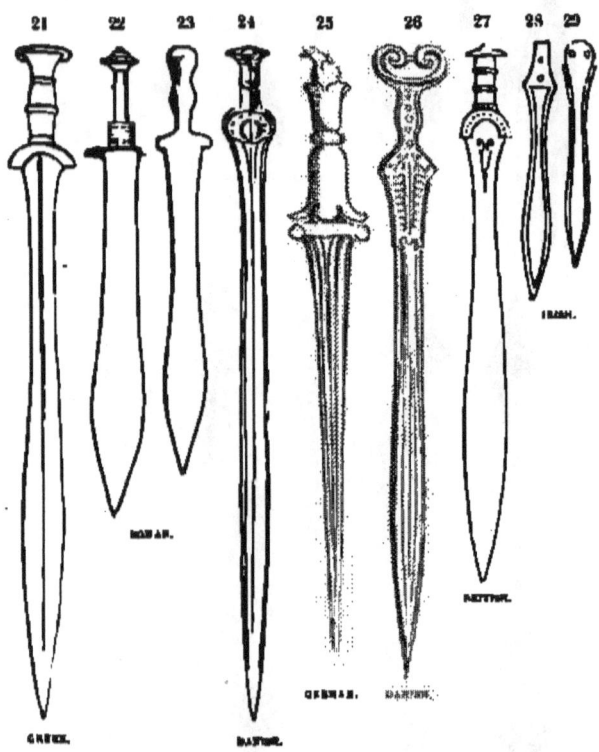

FROM "DEMMIN'S WEAPONS OF WAR."

plete sequence of development can also be traced from the bronze dagger, formed on the model of the flint dagger, with many intermediate forms, up to the fully developed leaf-shaped sword. They were evidently intended for stabbing and thrusting rather than for cutting.

Bronze swords, remarkable for their elegance of form and workmanship, are found in most parts of Europe. Everywhere, as Mr. Franks observes, they exhibit a great similarity of form, as though the weapons of one race; but in each country minute differences may be detected, which serve to show that they were not made in one place only, and exported to other lands.[*]

One chief difference between British and continental specimens is the general absence of the outer portions of the handle in one, and their presence in the other, owing to the more perishable material of which the former were made. The specimens found in Ireland are generally smaller than those from England. The largest sword in the Museum of the Royal Irish Academy measures twenty-nine and three-quarter inches in length; one from the Thames, of exactly the same type, is in the British Museum, and measures twenty-eight and six-tenths of an inch, but the

[*] "Horæ Ferales," p. 159.

AND BRONZE IMPLEMENTS.

No. 30.

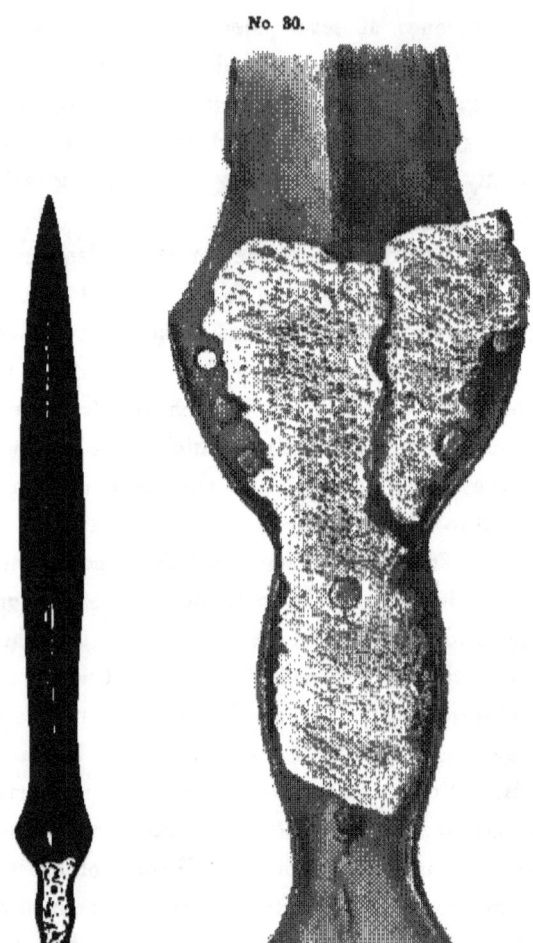

BRONZE LEAF-SHAPED SWORD WITH BONE HANDLE—IRELAND.

largest sword in the national collection is one from Battle, in Sussex, which measures twenty-nine and a half inches. Swords with complete bronze handles are rarely found in this country. In foreign examples, a bronze handle is of not unfrequent occurrence. In England and Ireland they had usually handles of wood or bone.*

The French examples are not unlike the English. In Denmark some of the swords closely resemble those from the British Isles. The generality of specimens, however, have elaborately ornamented handles; the largest of these swords seems to have been fully thirty-five inches in length. These types are likewise to be found in northern Germany. In Switzerland, the handles are generally more simple. The largest sword from Germany is thirty-six and three-quarter inches long. The ancient Greek and Roman bronze swords present the identical leaf-like shape of the British and Danish examples.

The ancient bronze implements and tools appear to be mere copies of the stone ones.

* Through the kindness of Mr. Day, I give a woodcut of a bronze leaf-shaped sword of beautiful form and proportions, which still retains a portion of the original bone handle. It is twenty-five inches long. It was found in Lisletrim bog, parish of Muckno, town land of Tullycoora, and barony of Cremorne, county Monaghan. It is now in the collection of Mr. Robert Day, F.S.A., Cork.

As Sir W. Wilde remarks, "In no other class of implements is the progress of development more truly represented, than in the gradual transition of the metal celt and palstave, from the rudest and simplest to the most perfect form."

We shall now follow Sir W. Wilde, and give the complete sequence of those bronze implements from the rudest and simplest form of the celt, which was evidently modelled on the type of the stone hatchet to the most perfect socketed form, and trace their process of development in the gradual transition of forms.

The term celt, from *celtis*, chisel, is quite conventional, but as it has been adopted more than a century ago to designate those weapon-tools in the shape of axes, hatchets, adzes and chisels, and preserved by authors since, it would be attended with much inconvenience to alter it now.

For the sake of arrangement, celts, although presenting more than a dozen varieties of form, may all be classed under three different heads: first, the plane hatchet-shaped piece of metal which passed into and probably through its wooden handle—this was denominated the *simple flat celt*; secondly, the winged celt or palstave, which mutually received, and was received into the handle; and thirdly, the *socketed celt*, in which the handle was inserted. These three varieties pass insensibly into each other. As this classification is founded on the mode of fixing these implements in their handles, he gives the following conjectural modes of hafting and using the metal celts.

Figure 31 represents a simple, flat, wedge-shaped celt, which passed through a wooden handle, and was

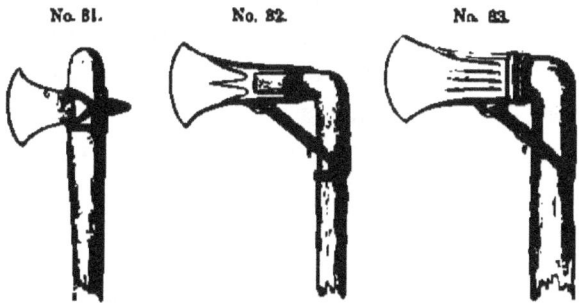

No. 81.　　No. 82.　　No. 83.

secured by a ligature possibly of hide or gut. By use, however, as a tool or weapon, it must in process of time have either split the handle or passed through it. A new plan was therefore adopted, that of making the metal and wood pass one into the other, and thus arose the winged celt or palstave. Here a curved piece of wood, like a hook, or ordinary crooked walking stick, was split or cut so as to receive the metal weapon, which had a slight wing or flange raised upon the lower edges of the narrow portion, to prevent its joggling or slipping up and down; and the parts thus adjusted must have been bound round after the fashion shown by No. 32.* That the winged celt had, however, originally no stop, is known by several examples discovered. Still a hard blow with this implement was apt to split the wooden handle, and so man's ingenuity devised a larger stop or elevated ridge, near the middle, at the junction between the axe blade, or cutting portion, and the parts which passed into and received the sides of the handle, against which they abutted. Nevertheless, the implement was imperfect, and still liable to split, and so, in process of time, the third great step in celt manufacture was achieved—that of making the metal the sole recipient of the wooden handle, by developing the wings, enlarging and bringing up the stop, and gradually removing the septum that divided the blade of the handle, until the implement became what is called a socketed celt, of which an example is given in the illustration, No. 33. This was a great step in advance, yet the implement was imperfect, because, as every person

* Mr. Kemble's description ("Horæ Ferales," p. 77) of the manner in which iron palstaves are hafted in Siberia, at the present day, would suggest a different mode of fixing them with a handle. See note at end of this chapter.

acquainted with the working of such tools is aware, it was apt to kick, the blade or cutting edge turning upwards at each repeated blow, until it finally flew off the handle, as any badly fitted hammer, hatchet, or adze would do. To obviate this defect, a loop was added to the lower edge, on both winged and socketed varieties, and to this was attached a stay either of metal or cordage, which occupied the angle between the celt and its handle where it was fastened ; thus the most perfect form of the implement was finally attained.

We shall now give a description of the various forms of the celts themselves, according to their progress of development.

The simplest form of celt is a cuneiform or wedge-shaped piece of metal, evidently formed on the type of the large stone celt; longer than it is broad, curved on its sharp-cutting, hatchet face, and square or rounded on the opposite narrow and blunted extremity. In length, this weapon varies from one inch long to upwards of twelve inches.

The winged celt or palstave presents the greatest variety of forms, showing most prominently the successive stages of its development. The first is a simple, narrow, chisel-edged celt (see Plate III., No. 4), in which the side edges project into flanges, so as to form

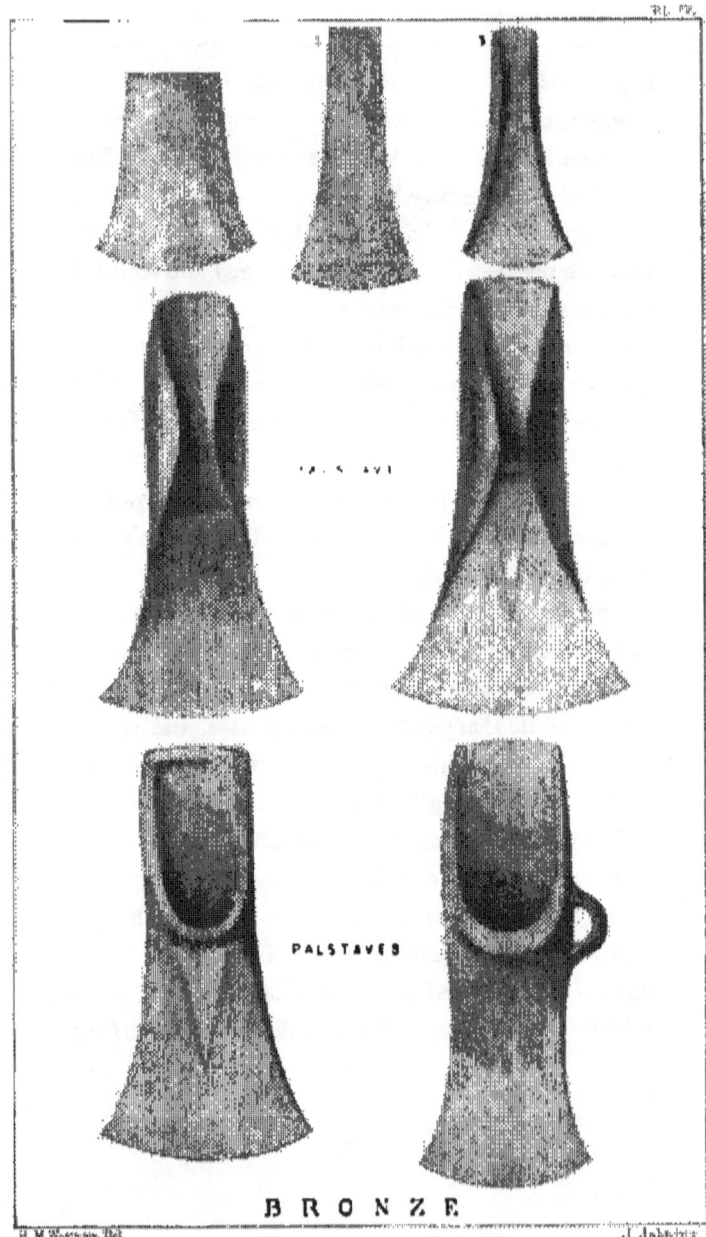

grooves for the reception of the cleft handle. The second form exhibits the wings, with the addition

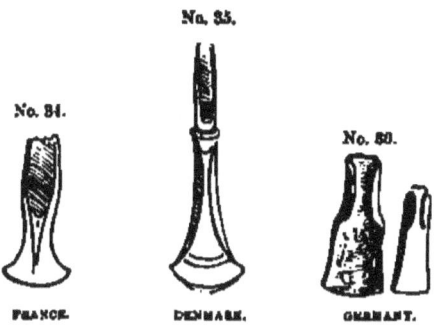

No. 35.

No. 34.

No. 36.

FRANCE.   DENMARK.   GERMANY.
PALSTAVES. From Demmin's "Weapons of War."

of a stop or elevated ridge near the middle (No. 5). In the third form (No. 6), the flange and stop were joined together, and thus assume the character of a socket with a septum or division, or rather two small side sockets, into which the wood passed; in this form we find a fourth variety (No. 7), where a loop was added, in order to secure the celt by a ligature to the haft.

By bringing up the stop a little more between the wings, in order to close the open of the latter, and at the same time removing the septum, the *socketed* or *recipient celt*, the final and complete form in the development of this implement was at once attained.

The cutting edge of the celts presents a great

diversity, from a very slightly curved line to that of the segment of a circle, the centre of which would be about the junction of the lower and middle thirds of

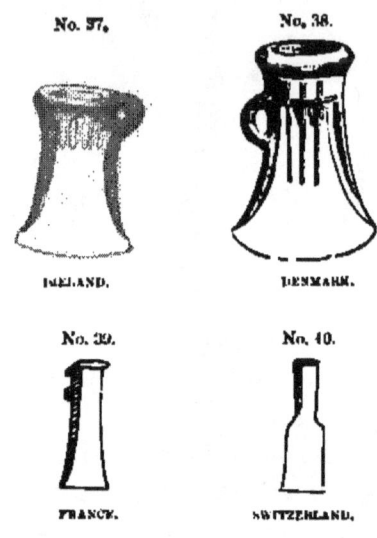

No. 37. No. 38.
IRELAND. DENMARK.
No. 39. No. 40.
FRANCE. SWITZERLAND.

SOCKETED CELTS. From Demmin's "Weapons of War."

the length of the instrument. In the simple axe-shaped celts, and also in the socketed variety, it is seldom much curved, and in some of the latter is almost straight. But in the palstave, or flanged celt, we find three well-marked varieties. The saddler's knife shape, in which the blade spreads out, sometimes to three times the width of the shaft; the lunette or semi-lunar form, the extremities sometimes forming hooked terminations; and the fan-shaped.

To secure the celt to the handle more effectually, a loop or eye was added in the casting to the inferior edge of both the winged and socketed celt, the object being evidently to provide against the flying off of the head, by securing it to the shaft by a stay between points where the greatest stress would come, when a heavy blow was given with the instrument, as already explained. In the palstave celt the loop is usually placed beneath the stop, and in the socketed one is always close to the top.

In the previous description may be traced the successive and uninterrupted development of the third and final variety of celt, from the simple, flat, wedge-shaped piece of metal, to the hollow implement formed to receive the end of the straight or crooked handle. As the stop became developed in the palstave variety, the enlarged wings merged into it, so as to form a socket on each side. From this there was but one step more, that of bringing up the stop between the sides of the wings, and removing the thin and gradually decreased septum, when the true socketed celt was achieved.

In external shape the socket presents several

varieties,—such as the circular, compressed or flattened, quadrangular, hexagon, and octagon. Some are long, narrow, square, chisel-edged, a type not uncommon in France.

. The cutting edge in the socketed celt is generally semi-lunar, although in some instances nearly straight, or chisel-shaped.

The top of the socket is generally ornamented, and very frequently surrounded by one or more raised bands or fillets.

In size the socketed celt runs from about one inch in length to five inches and one-eighth long. The smallest celt of any description, and possibly the least ever found in the British Isles, is in the Royal Irish Academy: it is six-eighths of an inch in length.

Bronze implements, showing a complete sequence of form, from the simple flat axe, to the socketed celt, have been discovered in many countries—in England, Ireland, Denmark, France, Italy,* Switzerland, and Germany—varying however somewhat in shape, form, and ornamentation, according to the country in which they were manufactured. A practical archæo-

* The figures of some Italian bronze celts, in my collection, on page 92, presenting examples of the three types, the flat, the winged, and the socketed, afford an interesting proof of the sequence of development of those bronze implements being independently carried out in Italy.

logist will readily distinguish the different peculiarities connected with each country.

That these bronze implements were the production and manufacture of the countries in which they are found, is proved by the moulds for casting them (Fig. 41), together with imperfectly cast specimens, being found in different countries—in England, Ireland, Denmark, Switzerland (Morges), France (Quetelot in Normandy), Hungary, Italy (near

No. 41.

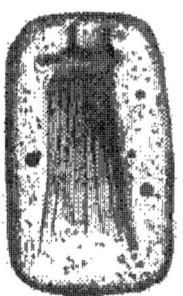

CELT MOULD—IRELAND.

Reggio). Moreover, as Mr. Franks observes, "Some minute variety of type or ornamentation is to be observed, which seems to demonstrate that the supply of such objects did not generally proceed from a common centre."

Implements and tools of bronze occur in Egypt, Chaldæa, and India.

92 ON THE SEQUENCE OF FLINT, STONE, COPPER,

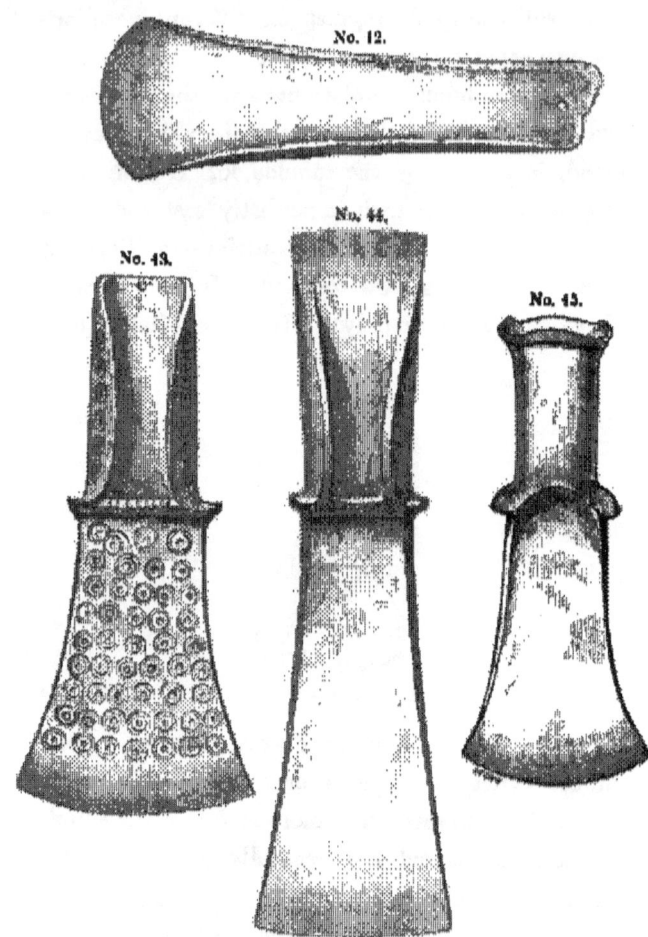

ITALIAN BRONZE CELTS, (half-size).

Bronze tools were also used by the Mexicans, and by the Peruvians, an important fact, as it attests the independent invention of that metal by these nations. "It is worthy of remark," Mr. Prescott says, "that the Egyptians, the Mexicans, and the Peruvians, in their progress towards civilization, should never have detected the use of iron, which lay around them in abundance, and that they should each, without any knowledge of one another, have found a substitute for it in such a curious composition of metals as gave to their tools almost the temper of steel." Nearly the same proportions result from the analysis of the bronze weapons found in the sepulchral barrows of Europe, of the instruments contained in the tombs of ancient Egypt, and of the tools of the Mexicans and Peruvians.

Humboldt brought back with him to Europe one of these metallic tools, a chisel found in a silver mine opened by the Incas, not far from Cuzco. On an analysis, it was found to contain 0·94 of copper, and 0·06 of tin.

The Mexicans derived their tin from the mines of Tasco, and their copper from the mountains of Zacatallan. The mountains of Peru abound in copper and tin.

The implements and weapons of the bronze age

are all cast. Those belonging to the more advanced stage of development show very considerable skill in metallurgy.

It has presented itself as a difficulty to many, how the ancients could have given sufficient hardness to comparatively so soft a metal as bronze, so as to carve and shape the hardest stones, a secret, it is said, that has been lost, or, to speak more correctly, has never been discovered by the civilized European. The following passage from Mr. Tylor's "Anahuac," may solve much of the difficulty. "When the subject of the use of bronze in stone cutting is discussed, as it is so often with special reference to Egypt, one may doubt whether people have not underrated its capabilities, when the proportion of tin is accurately adjusted to give the maximum hardness, and especially when a minute portion of iron enters into composition. Sir Gardner Wilkinson relates that he tried the edge of one of the Egyptian mason's chisels upon the very stone it had evidently been once used to cut, and found that its edge was turned directly; and therefore he wonders that such a tool could have been used for the purpose, of course supposing that the tool as he found it was just as the mason left it. This, however, is not quite certain. If we bury a brass tool in a damp place for a few weeks, it will be found to have undergone a curious molecular change, and to have become quite soft and weak, or, as workmen call it, dead. We ought to be quite sure whether lying for centuries under ground may not have made some similar change in bronze."

We have thus traced the gradual and progressive development of flint, stone, copper, and bronze implements in their transitional stages, and in their sequence of forms from the very rudest shape up to the most perfect socketed bronze type. This sequence affords an interesting and important proof of progress in the earliest phases of civilization, evinced in the ingenuity and skill, and in the adaptation of form to practical purposes displayed in those implements, by man in all countries in those early ages.

Addendum.

We can carry the sequence further into the iron age, when implements of iron were made in imitation of those of bronze. A remarkable discovery at Hallstadt, in Austria, has brought to light a transitional period, or a passage from the bronze to the iron age, when bronze tools were slowly dying out before the use of iron. The implements of iron found at Hallstadt, were actually copied from their predecessors in bronze. Bronze celts, faced with iron edges, were also found.

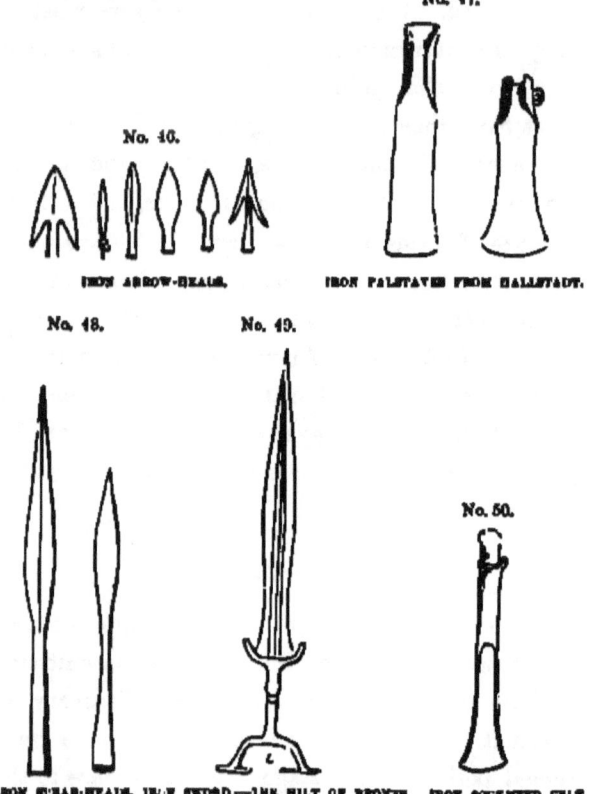

No. 16. IRON ARROW-HEADS.
No. 17. IRON PALSTAVES FROM HALLSTADT.
No. 18. No. 19. IRON SPEAR-HEADS. IRON SWORD.—THE HILT OF BRONZE.
No. 50. IRON SOCKETED CELT FROM HALLSTADT.

From Demmin's "Weapons of War."

The implements found at Marin, lake of Neufchatel,

show the iron implements following in strict sequence those of bronze. The specimens found there consist of weapons, of agricultural and domestic implements, and ornaments, and they exhibit to our view, made of iron, whatever, in older lake dwellings, was made of stone, or bone, or bronze.

The objects discovered in the lake dwelling of Marin, bring before us in the most prominent manner the iron age. It has been termed by antiquaries as pre-eminently the settlement of the iron age, when we reach the strictly historical period, and a more advanced phase of civilization.

Implements of iron carrying out the sequence of stone, bronze, and iron, have been also discovered in Denmark, England, France, and Germany.*

* Mr. Kemble in "Horæ Ferales," p. 77, in order to call attention to the importance of consulting the habits of those tribes, which are now in a similar state to that of our forefathers at the period when those weapons were in use, tells us, "Along the whole of the upper tract of Siberia the Mongol tribes are in the habit of carrying a weapon formed in every respect like our celts, both in the shape which we call socket, and that which, in imitation of our Danish friends, we have named palstave. The mode of fixing this with a handle is simple, but effective. A piece of bent wood, for which ash or blackthorn is admirably adapted, is fastened in the lower groove of the palstave; another piece of flat wood is placed within the upper groove; and the whole is then carefully wound round with the sinew of some animal; and thus is formed an implement, which, from personal experience, he can assure us, is capable

of dealing a most deadly blow. But a similar kind of the socket celt itself is found amongst the Gallo and Betuan tribes of Africa, differing in no conceivable point from the celt of our own forefathers, save in the material of which the implement is composed. In Africa, as in Siberia, it is of iron.

ON THE SEQUENCE OF THE PHASES OF CIVILIZATION, AND CONTEMPORANEOUS IMPLEMENTS.

It is familiar knowledge to us, that man in his progress through life, passes through the stages of infancy, childhood, youth, and manhood. There is evidence that man collectively passes through an analogous sequence in the stages of his development, the primitive barbarous, the hunting, pastoral, and agricultural phases. The last alone may be termed historic, as we frequently find a record of this phase in history, the other stages are pre-historic. On these, history is silent. The late wonderful discoveries in pre-historic archæology have opened up distinct vistas of the earliest pre-historic phases, the pastoral, the hunting, the rude and barbarous stages of separate races.

It appears as if there were but one history for

separate people, each passing through successive phases. As Figuier observes, "The development of man must have been doubtless the same in all parts of the earth, so that in whatever country we may consider him, man must have passed through the same phases, in order to arrive at his present state! He must have had everywhere his age of stone, his epoch of bronze, and his epoch of iron, in orderly succession."

The object of this chapter is not only to trace the sequence of these stages, in the development of man, but also to point out the various implements and weapons, which are contemporaneous and coincident with each phase. Of this view I shall now adduce a few proofs. In the first place, it must be admitted that the existence of these phases of civilization in each separate race, is undoubted, for all that has growth and progress advances by stages of development to a culminating point; and as it is impossible that they could be contemporaneous among the same people, they must have been successive, and in sequence, each phase ascending in progress from a ruder stage to a higher and more advanced one; analogous to the growth of the individual man, who cannot be an infant and youth, and a man at the same time, for these stages of his development are in him successive. The transition, however, from one phase to another was neither marked nor sudden, but a slow and gradual operation. There was thus an intermediate period, partaking of the lower and higher phases, and a blending of the two.

This law of sequence is evidently a prevailing law, not only in man, but in nature. Mr. Page thus expresses himself with regard to its observance in geology :— " The geological record is a thing of mere sequence, an inconceivable amount of unexpressed time, during which certain events follow each other in definite order."

In France, England, Italy, Sicily, Palestine, India, evidences have been discovered, of an early primitive barbarous phase, when man was contemporaneous with the mammoth and the woolly-haired rhinoceros, and used those large rude, flint implements, found in conjunction with the remains of those animals. The implements and weapons of this phase prove the man of that period to have been a savage of the lowest grade, unacquainted with the use of pottery, and even ignorant of the art of polishing or ornamenting the splinters of bone, or the rough flint that he used. Sir John Lubbock thus concludes on the evidence before him : " We may regard it as well-established, that the mammoth and woolly-haired rhinoceros co-existed with the savages who used the rude 'drift-hatchets,' at the time when the gravels of the Somme were being deposited."

Of the hunting stage of man's development, or that phase when flint arrow-heads and flint weapons were generally adopted, the North-American Indians, and the weapons used by them, afford proof that they lived by the chase, depending mainly on the animal kingdom for their subsistence. They were essentially hunters and fishermen; the buffalo, the deer, and the salmon supplying them with their principal articles of food; they exhibited an extraordinary amount of skill in the manufacture of their bows and arrows, and among several of the tribes, arrow making was a distinct profession. The arrow-heads, lance, spear-heads, such implements as would be used by a hunting people were, for the most part, of flint; in other countries, when flint was not available, they were manufactured of quartzite or obsidian. These implements were almost always chipped into shape. Distinct traces of this hunting stage, and the implements connected with it, have been discovered in France, England, Ireland, Denmark, Switzerland, America, and several other countries.

The sum of the evidence, from the discoveries of Mr. Lartet and Christy, proves that man, in a hunting state, lived in the south of France. On the floors of the caves discovered by them, fragments of the bones of the red deer, the chamois, the bouquetin, and more particularly the reindeer, have been found mixed up pell-mell with worked flints of different forms and sizes.

The Danish Kjökken-möddings were of this age. In those shell mounds, rude flint implements, sling stones, fragments of bone have been found. The primitive population of this period lived on the shore, and fed principally on shell-fish, but partly also on the proceeds of the chase.

A writer in the "Quarterly Review" makes the following observations on the grave mounds of the Yorkshire Wolds, which have yielded such a numerous crop of flint implements, and also some polished stone implements. "These grave mounds, the many foundations of huts that are found gathered into villages on the Cleveland moors, and elsewhere, and the remarkable dykes, and entrenchments that scar the sides of the wolds, and of the hills on the opposite side of the Vale of Pickering, are sufficient evidence that a somewhat numerous population of *hunters*, and perhaps of shepherds, dwelt on these high grounds for long ages before, and probably during the Roman occupation."

In Ireland, several hundreds of flint and chert implements, comprising arrow-heads of highly finished workmanship, scrapers, and other articles, together with bones, and a boar's tusk, have lately been found on a peninsula of Lake Ballyhoe; and the inference has been drawn, that red deer (their antlers are found in the lake), boars, and other wild animals, having been driven into this thickly wooded peninsula, were slain with these weapons on its shores by the ancient inhabitants who were hunters.

We find from Camden that the river Bann, on leaving Lough Neagh at Toom Castle, where at the present day flint flakes and flint arrow-heads are found in countless numbers, was beset and shadowed along the sides with woods, which were places of shelter for the wild Irish, who lived solely by the chase, and by fishing.

In a late excavation made by Dr. F. Keller, between Friedrickshafen, on the lake of Constance, and Ulm, the following objects were found: a number of small flint knives, and other implements of silex, in conjunction with the bones of the reindeer, of bears of large size, of the wolf, the ox, and also bones of birds, all evidences of a people who lived by the chase, and used those flint implements.

Implements of polished stone bear witness to a

more advanced stage of civilization, when man abandoning the more precarious mode of subsistence derived from the chase, learned to domesticate his prey, and reduce the wild animals around to his rule. He thus becomes a shepherd. Leading a more settled life, he builds for himself a dwelling, and learns to form implements more suited to his wants; he improves on the former rude shapes, grinds, polishes, and sharpens the stone implements which he will require for cutting timber, and for other purposes contributing to his need. The men of this stage possessed many useful arts; they invented the use of pottery, and were not ignorant of spinning; they dwelt in huts, the bottoms of which are now known as hut circles, sunk in the earth, or in dwellings raised on piles driven into shallow lakes. In Ireland the people of this age lived in raths or circular enclosures, which are generally met with in extensive pasture countries. The tumuli of Gaul, Germany, Britain, and Scandinavia, indicate their belief in a future state, and their reverence for the dead. They ground and polished their stone implements. Universally they had pressed the dog into their service. *They were essentially a pastoral people*, but lived also on the produce of the chase—the urus and the red deer, as well as upon their domestic animals, the horse, pig, sheep, goat, and short-horned ox.

Of the existence of this stage, and of the implements contemporaneous with it, there are proofs all over the world. Examples of ground and polished stone implements, almost identical in shape and form, have been found in different countries, and are witnesses of a similar phase of civilization, wherever found. That they were independently invented among these different peoples cannot admit of doubt.

The use of metal among any race makes an important era, and argues a more advanced stage of civilization. The introduction of more cutting instruments of metal must have led the men of that age to cut down forests, clear and till the ground, cultivate the soil, and consequently bring about a system of agriculture. The introduction of agriculture and metallurgy are generally announced as contemporaneous in ancient records. In Mexico and Peru, Quetzalcoatl and Manco Capac are said to have been the first who taught agriculture and metallurgy. The Pelasgi in Greece, who were an agricultural people, are said to have possessed a considerable knowledge of metallurgy. In Irish annals, the Tuath de Danaans are recorded as promoters of agriculture, and skilful metal workers. Late studies in the Vedas, show a bronze age among the Aryans, who were an agricultural people. The adoption of metal, however, was neither sudden nor universal, as the transition from the stone age to the bronze was slow and gradual. The earliest and simplest bronze celts were, as Sir W. Wilde remarks, "evidently formed on the type of the old stone celts;" these, however, were improved on until they assumed the more advanced forms, commonly termed the winged and socketed celts.

With regard to the connection of these bronze implements with the more advanced or agricultural stage, Sir John Lubbock comes to this conclusion:— "The evidence appears to show that the use of bronze weapons is characteristic of a particular phase in the history of civilization, and one which was anterior to the discovery, or at least to the general use, of iron," and, we may add, which was subsequent to the stone age. This phase was evidently the agricultural. Mr. Worsaae thus establishes the coincidence of bronze implements with an agricultural stage in Denmark. "The population, becoming possessed of useful metallic implements, began to till the earth. Having extirpated the forests in the interior of the country, partly by fire, partly by the axe, the inhabitants spread themselves over the whole land, and at the same time laid the foundation for an agriculture, which, up to the present day, is one of the principal industrial resources of Denmark." In Ireland the great antiquity of corn has been generally acknowledged, and sickles of bronze have been frequently obtained there.

At Camenz and Grossenhain, in Saxony, a number of bronze implements have been discovered, but the most important feature in the finds at both these places, is the number of bronze sickles they contained, proving an extensive cultivation of cereals, and consequently an evidence of an agricultural phase.

In regard to that part of Upper Italy, the Emilia, where there are traces of settlements of pre-Roman inhabitants, and where stone and bronze implements are found, Gastaldi remarks that these remains are proofs of various settlements which continued for a greater or less period of time. The nation was partly nomadic, such as shepherds and hunters, and partly stationary, such as fishermen and agriculturists.

Among the lake dwellings of Switzerland, some have been referred to the stone age, others to the bronze, as they exhibit a marked distinction in the implements found in them, and also in their fauna. The fauna of the former testifies to a pastoral people, the fauna of the latter to an agricultural people. Sir John Lubbock adduces evidences of the different phases of civilization, and their contemporaneous implements in the lake dwellings. Among those of the stone period, the list of objects found comprises seventeen axes, twenty whetstones, and ninety-seven arrow-heads, and flint flakes, while objects of metal are altogether absent, and but one doubtful case of a corn-crusher; on the other hand, in those of the bronze period, the large number of corn-crushers, and the presence of spinning weights are significant, and the total absence of stone axes is remarkable.

Bronze was used not for articles of luxury only, but also for the ordinary implements of daily life. The pottery tells the same tale. There is no evidence that the potter's wheel was known to men of the stone age, and the materials of which the stone age pottery is composed are very rough, containing large grains of quartz, while that of the bronze age is more carefully prepared. The ornaments of the two periods show also a great contrast. "Thus, then, we see," continues Sir John Lubbock, " that the distinction between the ages of stone and bronze is by no means confined to the mere presence of metal. The manufacture of pottery, the presence of the potter's wheel, the greater variety of acquirements, evidenced by the greater variety of implements, the indications of more advanced husbandry, the diminution of wild animals, and the increase of tame ones, all indicate a higher civilization for the inhabitants of Morges and Nidau (of the bronze age), than for those of Mooscedorf and Wauwyl (of the stone age).

Further Sir Charles Lyell confirms this view in his late work, "The Elements of Geology," p. 125; his words are: "The relative antiquity of the pile dwellings which belong respectively to the ages of stone and bronze, is clearly illustrated by the associations of the tools with certain groups of animal remains. Where the tools are of stone, the castaway bones which served for the food of the ancient people are those of the deer, the wild boar, and wild ox, which abounded when society was in the hunter state. But the bones of the later or bronze epoch were chiefly those of the domestic ox, goat, and pig, indicating progress in civilization."

A remarkable discovery at Hallstadt, in Austria, has brought to light a transitional period, or a passage from the bronze to the iron age, where bronze tools were slowly dying out before the use of iron. The arms of iron found at Hallstadt were actually copied from their predecessors in bronze. Bronze celts, faced with iron edges, were also found.

We have evidence of an iron age in connection with a more advanced phase of civilization on the borders of history. Proofs of this age are found throughout all Northern Europe. The lake dwelling of Marin, lake of Neufchâtel, brings before us in a most prominent manner the iron age. It has been termed by antiquaries as pre-eminently the settlement of the iron age. The specimens found there consist of weapons of agricultural and domestic implements, and ornaments, and they exhibit to our view, made of iron, whatever in the older lake dwellings was made of stone, or bone, or bronze.

Everything in this age evinces a higher culture.

Tacitus and Diodorus Siculus mention the Scots, and the Celts of Gaul, of their times, as using iron swords, and iron-headed spears.

In the iron age we thus reach a strictly historical period, and a more advanced stage of civilization.

To sum up, we may now conclude that there is evidence of a sequence of phases of civilization, and of contemporaneous implements among each separate race. A writer in a late number of the "Saturday Review" terminates his article in these words:—"In the scale of the former occupants of Western Europe we have, first, the flint folk of the geologist, then the reindeer folk in a hunter state, then the polished-stone-using folk (or pastoral), then the Celts, and lastly the Teutons." Sir John Lubbock at the end of his chapter on the Swiss Lake dwellings, and their inhabitants, observes:—" We have traced them through the ages of stone and bronze, down to the iron period. We have seen evidences of a gradual progress in civilization, and improvement in the arts, an increase in the number of domestic animals, and proofs at last of the existence of an extended commerce. We found the country inhabited only by savages, and we leave it the seat of a powerful nation." But of all countries, Denmark presents us with the most distinct evidences of a country passing through the flint, stone, and bronze ages in sequence, and the successive phases of civilization in connection with them. England, Ireland, and France also exhibit similar analogies in the developement of these successive periods.

This sequence of phases of civilization, it must be admitted, can be considered to exist alone among the races who have exhibited progress. Among the unprogressive races, such as the Negro, the New Zealander, the Australian, a blending, and sometimes a contemporaneousness of the same phases and implements, is visible; nor, indeed, was it always strictly followed out among the higher races, for, as Sir

John Lubbock acknowledges, "many stone implements belong to a metallic period." The presence, however, of stone implements, wherever found, bespeaks a want of civilization, and generally an ignorance of metals. In some remote and uncivilized parts, they have been retained even up to a late date. The Australians, and the South Sea islanders, at the time of their discovery, were still in the stone age, and evinced no signs of further progress. These races afford evidence of arrested development in their inability to advance beyond the stone age.

While admitting that the sequence of these phases is not always strictly followed out, it must not be imagined that there is any uncertainty with regard to the existence of this law of sequence; the few proofs we have given amply testify to it. It must be further kept in view, that the successive stages of civilization are not always contemporaneous in different countries. The period in time of any particular phase will depend entirely on the relative antiquity of the country in which these phases are evolved.

In conclusion, I may add that this view of the sequence of the phases of civilization among separate races, and the analogy in the forms of the implements used contemporaneously with them, may be considered as tending to prove an uniformity in the process of the development of man, and an analogy in the evolution of his natural instincts, and of the suggestive principle among all races; and further, as an emphatic proof of that orderly sequence which universally prevails in man and nature.

ON THE ANALOGOUS FORMS OF IMPLEMENTS AMONG EARLY AND PRIMITIVE RACES.

THE most remarkable feature in the early periods of man's history, is the almost identity—for it is more than a striking analogy—in the forms of the implements of warfare, and tools used in countries the most widely apart.* Man, in all ages, and in all stages of his development, is a tool-making animal. His instincts and necessities lead him to fashion implements and tools suited to his requirements. However different in race, and dwelling however remotely apart, we find in him the same wants and necessities; the same natural instincts and spontaneous powers of suggestion, contributing their aid in ministering to the needs of his nature, which he shares in common with

* This view when put forward some years ago in a paper read at the Anthropological Society was pooh-poohed as a wild speculation. It is now generally adopted, and has received the sanction of Professor Nilsson, Dr. Wilson, Mr. John Evans, and Mr. Darwin.

the whole human family. The same universal processes of mind and instinct will lead the Australian, the New Zealander, the Peruvian, the North American, the Scandinavian, and the ancient Briton to fashion and shape a stone weapon to supply his necessities and requirements.

A state of warfare was evidently the state of man in his earliest and barbarous stage. Combativeness appears to be the predominant instinct in man in his rude and savage state. Strifes and contests have grown up with human nature. Hatreds, jealousies, and rivalries have given rise to them in all ages. The present savage races are almost always at war. The New Zealanders were perpetually at war during life, and hoped to continue so after death. To form instruments of destruction to indulge his combative propensities, seems to have tasked the earliest powers of suggestion in man. Hunger and cold led him also to invent implements for the purposes of the chase, in order to supply himself with food, and a covering for his body, from the skins of animals.

The weapons and implements devised and fashioned by man in each stage of his development, are almost identical in all countries; for it does not admit of doubt, that men in a similar stage of civilization will devise and invent similar and identical objects. As

Dr. Keller remarks, "A similar state of civilization always calls for similar wants, and then again for similar means to supply them, and consequently similar implements, for the different purposes of life."* This similarity affords strong evidence of the uniformity of the operations of instinct, and the suggestive principle in the mind of man, among all races, and in all ages.

These warlike and useful implements present identical forms according as we consider them under the different epochs of flint, stone, bronze, or iron; and this sequence in the forms of the implements adopted during these successive periods, which are evidently worked out independently among different races, is obviously the result consequent on the progress or the development of man, which proceeds uniformly among all races. For there is evidence that all nations, in these earlier times, have proceeded in an invariable sequence through the periods of flint, stone, and bronze, ages before they arrived at the more advanced iron age.

* Mr. John Evans also adopts this view. His words are: "This parallelism of type seems to afford most remarkable proof that the same wants, with the same means at command for fulfilling them, result, so far as tools are concerned, in the production of similar forms, no matter where or when the men live who make them."—*Review of the Transactions of the International Congress of Prehistoric Archæology in "Nature."*

The earliest known forms of weapons used either for purposes of warfare, or the chase, are the implements found in the gravel drift. It has been remarked, that the characteristic of these worked flints is their striking resemblance to each other, in almost every country where they have been found. They present identical forms, obviously the result of identical intention. The flint implements of the gravel drift found in England, exhibit the same distinctive features peculiar to those found at Abbeville, and St. Acheul, in France. Implements of the same type, and of identical forms, have been found in Spain, Assyria, and in India.* They are of the rudest nature, as if formed by a people in the most degraded state of barbarism. According to Mr. Evans, "the flint weapons found in conjunction with elephant remains, imbedded in gravel, overlaid by sand and brick-earth, present no analogy to the well-known implements of the so-called Celtic or stone

* Mr. Bruce Foote remarks with regard to the quartzite implements of palæolithic type, from the laterite formation of the east coast of southern India. "I have since the beginning of this year had the opportunity of seeing several of the best collections of flint implements from the drift, including those of Mr. John Evans, the Blackmore Museum, Mr. Prestwich, Mr. J. W. Flower, and Mr. James Wyatt; and I think I may safely say that I could, from among the hundreds of quartzite implements that I have collected and studied, find a close match for nearly every form in those rich collections."

period. They have appearances of having been fabricated by another race of men, and on a much larger scale, as well of ruder workmanship." They are thus evidences of a very early, perhaps the earliest, stage of development, and of an age of ruder strength and still more infantine skill; perhaps, too, of an earlier species of human-like race, the companion and contemporary of the extinct bear, the extinct rhinoceros, the mammoth, and other larger animals, no longer in existence.

The next period is the stone age. Flint and stone implements are found in all countries, and are thus witnesses of a period of early and imperfect civilization. They are the most simple implements, such as would be suggested to man in his primitive and barbarous state, either as destructive instruments for supplying himself with food by the chase, and for warfare or defence; or as useful implements for cutting timber, for constructing habitations, or forming boats or rafts. Flint and stone implements are found among all primitive nations throughout the world, whose maintenance chiefly depended on their energy and ingenuity while unacquainted with the harder metals. The men who adopted flint implements were evidently a hunting people, who lived solely by the proceeds of the chase, and consequently in one of the earliest stages of the human race, as is shown by the partly devoured bones of the urus, the deer, the megaceros, the roe, found in connection with them. The desire to attack his enemies from a greater distance, and to engage in the chase, has suggested to man, in this early age, the use of the arrow. Hence, arrow-heads of flint or stone are found in all countries where a hunting phase of civilization prevailed; and this we may add was nearly all over the world.* Their striking resemblance is also very remarkable: the arrow-heads of flint found in America, are scarcely distinguishable from those found in Ireland. We take the following passage from Captain Mayne Reid, which confirms our view that a natural instinct will lead men to the independent invention of bows and arrows, as well as to the adoption of identical forms of arrow-heads, in countries the most widely apart. "The use of the bow among savage nations all over the earth, and the great similarity of its form and construction everywhere, may be regarded as one of the most curious facts in the history of our race. Tribes and nations that appear to have been isolated beyond all possible communication with the rest of the world, are found in possession of this universal weapon, constructed on

* See Plate I.

the same principle, and only differing slightly in detail, these details usually having reference to surrounding circumstances. When all else between two tribes or nations of savages may differ, both will be found carrying a common instrument of destruction —the bow and arrow. Can it be mere coincidence like necessities in different parts of the world, producing like results?"*

The stone implements of countries the widest apart present also analogous forms.† The stone axe of the South Sea islanders of the eighteenth century presents a close resemblance to that of British or Gaulish fabrication of the earliest centuries. In form there is little to distinguish the stone celts found in India from those which are so frequently found in Europe. Many Asiatic celts might be matched with specimens found in Ireland.‡

* An extraordinary similarity is also found in the way in which the bow and arrow is used in widely apart countries. A Fan bowman, in Africa, as described by Du Chaillu, and a Caboclo archer, as figured in Messrs. Kidder and Fletcher's "Travels in Brazil," in regions so remote as to preclude all idea of intercommunication, shoot in exactly the same manner, by applying both feet to the middle of the bow, which they pull with all strength on the string to bend it back.

† See Plate II.

‡ One of the most extraordinary coincidences is, that the same term is applied to these stone celts by the ignorant peasantry of the different countries in which they are found. In Brittany, they

A mass of evidence proves that a stone age prevailed in every great district of the inhabited world. Stone implements are found in countries the most widely apart, and are not peculiar to any race, but are naturally suggested to any race of men in a rude and imperfect stage, and are peculiar to that stage alone. They are found in Scandinavia, Britain, Ireland, France, Italy, Greece, Spain, Asia, America, Africa, Japan, Tenerife, New Zealand, Australia, and the South Sea Islands; all, whether modern or thousands of years old, presenting a marked uniformity. As Professor Worsaae remarks, "The weapons and instruments of stone which are found in the north of Europe, in Japan, in America, the South Sea Islands, and elsewhere, have, for the most part, such an extraordinary resemblance to one another in point of form, that one might almost suppose the whole of them to have been the production of the same maker. The reason of this is very obvious, namely, that their form is that which first and most naturally suggests itself to the human mind."

In the next age, the manufacture of bronze weapons

---

are styled "pierres de tonnere." In Italy, "pietre di fulmine." In Germany, "Donnerkeile." In Greece, "ἀστροπελέκια." In China, "lightning-stones." In Japan, "thunderbolts, Rai fu-seki." In India they are supposed to have fallen from heaven.

may be considered as a further improvement on the fabrication of stone implements, consequent on the knowledge of the harder metals, the improvement corresponding with the grade attained to in civilization. Adopting the words of Professor Wilson, we may say that "the same rational instinct which prompted man in his first efforts at tool-making, guided him in a discriminating choice of materials, and to this, the discovery of metals, and the consequent first steps in metallurgy, and the arts may be traced." The adoption of metal, however, was neither sudden nor universal. The transition from the rude implements of stone, to those of bronze, must have been very gradual, and possibly extended over many centuries. The bronze implements and weapons peculiar to this epoch, found in Egypt, Denmark, England, Ireland, Italy, France, Spain, and America, also bear distinct analogies in form to one another. As Sir William Wilde observes, "Like its predecessors in stone, the metal celt had a very wide distribution, and has been found in every country in Europe, from the river Tiber to the Malar Lake, but differing slightly in shape and ornamentation from those found in the British Isles." Like the stone implements, they are not peculiar to any race, but are suggested to any primitive nation, as a necessary result of an invariable sequence in its progressive development. We may add, adopting Professor Worsaae's words, "The antiquities belonging to the bronze period, which are found in the countries of Europe, can neither be attributed exclusively to the Celts, nor to the Greeks, Romans, Phœnicians, Scandinavians, nor to the Teutonic tribes. They do not belong exclusively to any people, but have been used by the most different nations *at the same stage of civilization*." We must remark, that, however like in form these implements seem to common observers, still there are distinctive characteristics, however slight, of each race in each type of implement, easily distinguished by the practised eye.

Further, besides remarking the obvious analogy of form in their bronze implements in different countries, it is also remarkable that nearly the same proportions (ten or twelve per cent of tin), result from the analysis of the bronze weapons found in the sepulchral barrows of Europe, of the nails which fastened the plates with which the treasury of Atreus at Mycene was covered, of the instruments contained in the tombs of ancient Egypt, and of the tools of the Mexicans and Peruvians, the same powers of suggestion in man, operating alike in all countries, and leading him not only to the discovery and fabrication of like forms of weapons, but also to the invention and use of similar materials.

The simplest form of bronze implement is a cuneiform or wedge-shaped piece of metal, evidently modelled on the type of the large stone implements; at a later period it assumes a more ornamental form, or a shape better suited for being attached to the wooden handle with which it was used, as in the so-called " winged celts, or " palstaves " in Ireland or Denmark. The earlier form of implement was merely inserted in the handle, and sometimes tied to it. Palstaves of almost identical forms—or those bronze implements in which the side edges project into flanges so as to form grooves for the reception of the cleft handle— are found in many countries, in Denmark, England, Ireland, France, Switzerland, Germany, Hungary, Etruria, and Magna Græcia, each of these countries exhibiting evidences of a sequence of flint, stone, and bronze period. The period of the similarity of the weapons or implements in these countries, in their stone and bronze ages, being always according to the stage of development of the race or country in which they are found, and not always according to any fixed or certain period of time. We thus find confirmed the inference that man's inventive and suggestive faculties, operating alike in each stage of his development and in all races of men, will lead him, independently and without connection, to fashion and invent, under similar circumstances and according to that stage, almost similar weapons and implements to supply his wants and necessities, each style of implement being peculiar to, and belonging exclusively to, each separate period or phase of civilization.

In a later age, when iron was known and generally adopted, the earlier forms of instruments were still retained for some time, until the rapid progress of civilization and refinement caused them to be thrown aside. In Denmark, at Marin in Switzerland, and at Hallstadt in Austria, iron implements have been found, exact copies of their predecessors in bronze. Iron, however, once known, advancement was rapid. We need not speak further of the iron age, as it is not peculiar to early and primitive nations, but is evidence of an advanced and more perfect state of civilization, and a progress towards the culminating period of man's development, when higher suggestive and inventive faculties were brought into play.

ON THE TRIBAL SYSTEM AND LAND-TENURE IN IRELAND, UNDER THE BREHON LAWS.

In order to illustrate the tribal system which generally prevailed during the pastoral phase, I here give a view of the system as it obtained in Ireland during the pastoral stage in that country, drawing largely from Mr. Richey, and an article on the Brehon Laws in the "Penny Cyclopædia."

The social condition of the early Irish people was patriarchal and pastoral. The Brehon laws, which enable us to realize that society in its pre-historic state, and the frequent number of the *raths*, or homesteads, enclosed by a ditch and rampart for the protection of flocks and herds in the wide pasture grounds, amply testify to this.

Prior to the Anglo-Saxon invasion, Ireland was solely governed by the Brehon law, so-called from being expounded by judges named in the Irish language, *Breitheamhuin* or *Brehons*. *Feinachas*, however, and

Breitha-neimeadth, words signifying respectively ancient laws and sacred ordinations, are terms commonly applied to the collection of the ancient laws of the Irish by the native writers. There is abundant evidence to prove that some of the collections of the Breitha-neimeadth are of equal antiquity with the oldest manuscripts of Irish history, whether civil or ecclesiastical,—an antiquity which carries us safely back to the earlier ages of the Christian era. The language in which they were written has become obsolete; and two successive commentaries remain, written themselves in two successive antiquated dialects. They evince, it is true, a very primitive state of society, but still they are, for the greater part, the work of Brehons, conformable to Brehon law, and afford indisputable evidence that the native Irish not only possessed a fixed and written code by which to regulate the judgments of their Brehons, but also that these functionaries duly committed their judgments, such as they were, to writing. Archbishop Usher speaks of the Brehon laws as being in his day contained " in large volumes, still extant in their own [the Irish] language." A collection, which now fills two large quarto volumes, is deposited in the library of the Royal Irish Academy. They are now in course of publication by the Government.

The following is a brief notice of the social system and land-tenure of the old Irish under the Brehon laws, such as their available fragments, compared with the general history of the country, would point out to the reader of the various accessible authorities on the subject.

It is well known that Irish society was formed upon the tribal system. The tribe system is the primitive state of society, the first shape into which human society is moulded, and the first step towards the agglomeration of nations. It arises from the condition and necessities of the earliest wanderers: " The tribe may be defined as the intermediate degree in the social scale between the family and the nation. When a family extends itself beyond the limits of consanguinity, embracing a relatively wider sphere, it is naturally transformed into a tribe. The ties of affection and habit which cement union between the members of the same family get weakened with the extension of the family circle, and are then replaced by the ties of tradition, of worship, and of common interests. Then the numerous members of the widely spread family form a mass which receives the denomination of tribe."*

Most nations may be traced back to this primitive

* Major Millengon. " Wild Life among the Koorls," p. 282.

form, and it still subsists over a large portion of the world. The tribe-system is the development of the family. The first wanderer from the original seat of the people strays forth into foreign lands at the head of his family: the father is at once the priest, the judge, and the king. He rules his children, as the ablest and the wisest; round the original family gather their slaves and dependants. All the members of the original family and their followers form a single unit. No individual has an existence except as a member of this body; their flocks and herds form a common property. They possess no clear idea of individual ownership. The tribe exists upon the assumption of common descent.

Suppose a tribe of this nature to abandon its wandering life, and conquer for itself a district in some foreign country; the principles upon which the land would be occupied flow from the ideas on which the tribe is constituted. The tribe is an undivided whole. The land would be conquered by all for the benefit of all, and would belong to all in common. For the convenience of cultivation, separate lots might be appropriated to individuals, but none would gain an absolute ownership in his allotted portion. His occupancy would be subject to resumption by the tribe; and the arable land might be from time to time divided, as would suit the convenience of all. The pasture-lands would remain open for the cattle of the tribe, subject to such rules as from time to time might be thought necessary.

Most of this system we find developed in Irish tribal history. The districts occupied by an Irish tribe generally amounted to about the area of a modern barony, and belonged, as a rule, to the tribe. This common land seems to have been divided into common pasture-land, common tillage-land, private demesne-land, and demesne-land of the tribe ; each man of the tribe had a right to pasture as many cattle as he possessed on the common grazing-land ; and in proportion to the number of cattle thus pastured by each, was the share of the common tillage-land assigned to him upon the annual partition. The private demesne-lands were the distinct property of individuals, who were entitled to acquire and transmit by certain qualifications not very clearly explained. The demesne-lands of the tribe were set apart for the maintenance of the chief elect or tanist, the bard, the doctor, and Brehon ; the four offices of the chief, bard, doctor, and Brehon were descendable in distinct families, but not necessarily from father to son, rather the contrary. Upon his demesne-lands the chief established his tenants, many of them not members of the tribe; he thus provided for his military followers, whom he also had a right of quartering from time to time on the members of the tribe itself.

With regard to the nature of the property enjoyed in these several estates, the tribe at large possessed what is called the allodial or original indefeasible property in all the lands, *and could not be ejected out of them in consequence of any arrears of tribute*, inasmuch as the superior lord claimed only a proportion of the increase of stock upon the pastures, and was bound to take the same away at certain seasons; this rent was precisely a lay-tithe, being one-tenth of the increase. As to the common tillage-lands, every member of the tribe possessed a life-interest in them, proportioned to his stock in cattle. In the private demesne-lands individuals had a permanent inheritable interest. In his separate portion of the demesne-lands of the tribe, the chief had a life-interest, of which the reversion lay with the tanist, *i.e.* the *second-man*, or chief-elect; and in like manner the tanist, bard, &c., possessed life-interest in their several portions.

The distinctions of the tribe, corresponding to the above territorial divisions, were, so far as can be gathered from the confused authorities on this head, the *In-finnè*, holders in common, and the *Dathaig-finnè*,

those individuals alluded to above who were entitled
to separate inheritable possessions. The *In-finnè*, or
commonalty of this pastoral corporation, appear to
have been of one rank; but the *Dathaigh-finnè* were
divided into several classes, of which the three most
intelligible were, the *Deirbh-finnè*, or class, as the
commentators explain it, nearest to succession, who
had the right to inherit the whole patrimony of their
kin without deduction; the *Gall-finnè*, who inherited
three-fourths of their patrimonial estates; and *Sar-
finnè*, whose right of inheritance extended to only
one-fourth of the property left by their relations.
These privileged classes were, in every tribe, limited
in number; but it does not exactly appear what was
the qualification for admission, or the rule of exclu-
sion, or whether the *Deirbh-finnè*, for instance, became
disqualified on the election of a tanist less nearly
related to them than to others; although it is evident
that a man might rise from the condition of a tenant
of common tillage to that of a freeholder, or, *vice
versâ*, descend from the higher class to the lower.
As to the chief himself, he was usually elected before
the death of his predecessor, and the rule seems to
have been invariably that the eldest of the candidates,
if not incapacitated by age or infirmity, should have
the preference, the brother being commonly chosen

instead of the son, and the son rather than the
nephew. His revenue arose, as has been said, from
the tenths of the increase of cattle, and from the
revenues of his demesne-lands. In addition, he had
certain claims of entertainment for himself and house-
hold, at stated times, in the houses of his tenants, in
the same manner as his superiors, at certain seasons,
quartered themselves or their soldiers upon him.
These claims were sometimes compromised by both
for an equivalent in tribute.

So far of the *Finnè*, or original members of the
kindred, who constituted the great majority of the
tribe. But in every tribe there was another class,
less numerous and generally less honourable, but
in many respects peculiarly interesting and important,
particularly as regards the origin of the *feudal law*.
The subject of feudal tenures has occupied the attention of the most distinguished English lawyers and
historians. The origin of the system has been in all
cases referred more or less to the necessities of military
conquest, and its genius has been invariably considered as quite distinct from that of any pastoral
constitution. The remains of the Brehon law, however, would go far to show that the feudal and
pastoral systems, if not to some extent identical, have
been in their origin closely and necessarily connected.

The system laid down above is so far calculated for the government of a society composed of tribes, each tribe possessing the allodium of its own district, and the mass of its members holding in common. But coexistent with the first practical development of such a system, if not actually contemplated in its very rudiments, arises the necessity of providing for those members of the community who, either by chance, or choice, or compulsion, have been separated from their particular kindreds, and have thus no proper *Finné* with whom to claim a share. Such individuals could not expect to participate in the rights of blood enjoyed by those tribes among which they might be dispersed, neither could they be received by the commonalty of those tribes as tenants on their fluctuating possessions. To provide for them, it was necessary that a certain portion of the land should be set apart for the reception of strangers. To prevent the confusion of many lordlords, the profits of these tonements were allotted to the chief, who could thus afford to exact a higher tribute from the *Finns* of his tribe. To induce the better sort of strangers to settle among them, the chief was empowered to grant some of these tenements in perpetuity; but the greater portion was usually let at will. As for those who had only their labour to offer in lieu of the chief's protection, they were received on his private demesne-lands and became his serfs. Admission to the upper class depended on the stranger's ability to pay the entrance-fee on one or more of the disposable tenements. These tenements consisted of a homestead, with a certain extent of ground annexed: the homestead was denominated a *Rath*: to constitute a legitimate rath, five things were requisite, viz., a dwelling-house, an ox-stall, a hog-sty, a sheep-pen, and a calf-house; these buildings were generally surrounded by a ditch and rampart, and formed, if necessary, a place of defence as well as residence.*

---

* A similar phase of civilization has led to the formation of a similar mode of dwelling among the Todas, a wild aboriginal tribe of the Nilgiri Hills in India. Colonel W. Ross King thus describes the dwellings of the Todas: "The roof is made of reeds, and thatched with common grass. The whole structure is very substantially and neatly built, but there is no chimney, and the smoke from the fire pours out at the door, and exudes from every crevice. The entrance is an opening just sufficient to admit a full-grown person on hands and knees, and is made to close from within. There is in front of the dwellings, partly enclosed by a low wall of loose stones, an open grassy space or court, which, owing to the nomadic habits of the Todas, is always of a fresh green. The huts are built close together on some naturally smooth knoll, in clusters of three or four only, and not in villages; these family groups are called *munds*. Each mund has an enclosure, or pen, called a *tooel*, in which the buffaloes are confined at night; it is generally circular in form, and consists of a low wall of loose stones surrounding a sunk area within.

There is one very prevalent error with regard to raths in Ireland, viz., that they were Danish erections, and designed solely for military occupation. The term "Danish rath" is altogether a misnomer. The original titles of raths, according to the classification of the Brehon law, were drawn solely from the circumstance of their erection and occupation by the natives themselves,—as, for example, among many others, the *Finnè-rath*, a homestead occupied by the

---

There is always one hut set apart for the reception of milk, and this placed a little to one side of the other huts, which in construction it precisely resembles. The *wunds* are situated at considerable distances apart, and their inhabitants migrate periodically from one to another for change of pasture.

A similar mode of life peculiar to the pastoral phase has been observed among the Guachos, an uncivilized tribe of Indians. They are thus described: "These native Guachos are possessed of vast herds of wild cattle, and roam over the country in a state of semi-savage independence. Their dwellings are constructed of wicker-work, with a hole in the roof for the escape of smoke. An enclosure for cattle adjoins the hut, and the whole is surrounded by a fence of impenetrable cactus."

The earth enclosures in North America would also seem to bespeak a similar phase of civilization.

From Cæsar we learn that what the Britons call a town, is a tract of woody country, surrounded by a vallum and a ditch for the security of themselves and their cattle against the incursions of their enemies. Analogous enclosures which served as homesteads are found among other races. Among the Ovambos, an African tribe, their houses are placed in an enclosure, the best being for the master and his immediate family, and the others

original kindred; a *Mer-rath*, one rented by stranger tenants for the first time; a *Sar-rath*, one occupied by stranger serfs on the chief's demesne-lands. The entrance-fine of such a tenement was denominated *fal*, and, for the legitimate rath, amounted to fifty head of cattle. As distinguished from the Finnè, or original clansmen, the stranger-tenant was called *Fuidhir*, and his tenure *Fuidh*. These terms are pronounced respectively *Feuer* and *Feu*.

Thus, then, it would appear, that the country was

---

for the servants. There are besides grain stores, houses for cattle, fowl-houses, and even sties for pigs, one or two of these animals being generally kept in each homestead, though the herds are rigidly excluded. Within the same enclosure are often to be seen a number of ordinary Drogermen huts. These belong to members of that strange tribe, many of whom have taken up their residence with the Ovamboa, and live in a kind of relationship with them, partly considered as vassals, partly as servants, and partly as kinsfolk.

The Kaffir kraal, a circular enclosure, bears also a close analogy to these same homesteads.

Mr. E. H. Palmer (Desert of the Exodus, p. 321), describes similar enclosures among an Arab pastoral tribe:—"When a camping ground has been selected, the cattle, as the most precious possession of the tribe, are collected together in one place, and the huts or tents are pitched in a circle round them; the whole is then fenced in with a low wall of stones, in which are inserted thick bundles of acacia. These are called *Dowârn*, and there can be but little doubt that they are the same with the *Hazeroth* or 'fenced enclosures' used by pastoral tribes mentioned in the Bible."

occupied by kindreds called *Finnè*, holding for the
most part in common, and by *Feuers*, who were
either tenants by rent and service, or vassals of the
chief. The tributes of chief to superior chief, up to
the supreme king of the whole island, were regulated
by established precedents. The collection of these
rules for the kingdom of Munster is entitled "The
Book of Rights," and is still extant.

It has been seen above that in proportion to the
number of cattle possessed by each member of the
tribe was his share of the common tillage-lands.
Thus cattle were not only the standard of value, but
the qualification for, and a necessary concomitant of
property. The land was thus, by a sort of legal
fiction, an appurtenance of the stock; so that to say
of a person under this system, that he possessed a
hundred cows, implied not only that his herds
amounted to so many head of cattle, but that in
addition, and as a necessary appurtenance of his
estate in them, he also possessed the *grazing* of a
hundred cows, and the share proportioned to a
hundred cows in the common tillage-lands of his
tribe. Every addition to the number of a man's
cattle was therefore a virtual accession of land and
produce, and *vice versâ*; and thus a mulct of cattle
fell as heavily on the granary, as on the larder or

dairy of the fined individual; for these proportionate partitions of the land took place at stated periods, and each man's harvest fluctuated with his herds, as they bore a greater or less ratio to the aggregate of all the cattle of the rest. The division of the ground into portions so uncertain, precluded the use of permanent fences on those arable commons, which were probably separated from the pasture by only one exterior circumvallation, while each man knew the portion that was to fall to his reaping-hook within. The adjustment of these portions must have been a matter of some difficulty. It would appear that the plan usually formed was this:—The land was divided into equal shares, in the proportion, each to the whole, of the herd of the least proprietor to the whole *creaght*, or common stock of all their cattle. These shares were drawn by lot, in order to give to all an equal chance of getting the worse or better land. He thus, it is supposed, whose herds were thrice as numerous as those of the least proprietor, drew three such aliquot parts; he possessing ten times as many, ten such, and so on, the shares being taken here and there, as they turned up, and every man cropping his own portion as he thought fit. The system is still remembered in some parts of the country, and a mode of expressing the extent of land among the Munster peasantry is still to say "so much as *follows* so many cows;" hence in all likelihood, the term *Bally-boe, e.i.*, "cow-land," a term which has perplexed many writers, in consequence of the varying extent represented by it at different times and in different districts.*

Such, so far as can be collected from the present ill-arranged and defective materials, would appear to

* The pastoral phase appears to have been of long continuance in Ireland, and to have prevailed even to a late period. We give the two following illustrative extracts. "At the same time (A.D. 606), the mass of the Irish population was little advanced beyond the nomad state, a condition of society which in some districts of Ireland was maintained for many succeeding centuries. When Ulster, south and west of Lough Neagh came to be finally subdued by Queen Elizabeth's forces under Lord Mountjoy in 1603, and James I. resolved to effect the plantation of it with colonists from Scotland and England; one of the greatest difficulties met with was, how to render amenable to law and order the pastoral population, which from early ages had been accustomed to wander without any fixed habitations after their herds of cattle, living almost solely on white meats, as the produce of their cows was called. At this period there was not one fixed village in all the country, a circumstance we learn incidentally from Sir John Davis' letter to the Earl of Salisbury, written during the first circuit ever held in Fermanagh, when he mentions that "the fixing a site for a jail and session house had been delayed until my lord deputy had resolved on a fit place for a market and corporate town," for, he adds, "the habitations of this people are so wild and transitory, as there is not one fixed village in all this country." Their dwellings are described as made of wattles or boughs of trees, covered with long turves or sods of grass, which

have been the old tribal system and land-tenure which prevailed in Ireland prior to the invasion of the Anglo-Normans in the twelfth century. The Brehon law, however, prevailed in every part of Ireland not immediately subject to the English power until the reign of James I., when the ancient Irish laws were abolished.

they could easily remove and put up as they wandered from place to place in search of pasture. The aggregate of families that in one body followed a herd was called a "creaght."—*The Ulster Creaghts*, by J. Prendergast, "*Kilkenny Journal*."

Giraldus Cambrensis observes that in his time "the Irish nation lives on the produce of their cattle, and leads a life but little superior to them, nor have they emerged from the pastoral state. As the progress of human society is to advance from woods to open fields, and from the latter to towns, this nation despising agriculture, inattentive to civil wealth, and regardless of law, spend their lives in woods and pastures."

ON CROMLECHS AND MEGALITHIC STRUCTURES.

It is now a generally accepted canon that there are common instincts implanted by nature on all the varieties of the human race, which lead mankind in certain climates, and at a certain stage of civilization, to do the same thing in the same way, or nearly so, even without teaching, or previous communication with those who have done so before. This has been remarkably confirmed in the analogous and almost identical forms of flint and stone implements all over the world; and also in the identity of ornamentation, such as the zigzag, guilloche, etc., designed independently by races the most widely apart.

A further confirmation of this, are the analogous modes of burial, almost identical in their forms in different parts of the world.

Man, in his early and rude stage, will adopt the simplest mode of burial suggested to him. The tumulus or mound of earth, the simplest and earliest form, is therefore found wide spread among all peoples. As Sir John Lubbock says :—" In our island they may be seen in almost every town. In the Orkneys alone, it is estimated that more than two thousand still remain; they are found all over Europe, from the shores of the Atlantic to the Ural mountains; in Asia, they are scattered over the great steppes, from the borders of Russia to the Pacific Ocean, and from the plains of Siberia to those of Hindostan ; in America, we are told that they are to be numbered by thousands and tens of thousands. Nor are they wanting in Africa, where the pyramids themselves exhibit the most magnificent development of the same idea: so that the whole world is studded with burial places of the dead."

A further improvement on the simple mound we find among the Etruscans, who surrounded the base with a podium or supporting wall of masonry. Of this kind of tumulus, or conical mound, examples occur in immense numbers in every necropolis of Etruria. We find the same form in the tumulus of Tantalus near Smyrna, in the tomb of Alyattes at Sardis, in the Buddhist topes of India, and in Chinese tombs, which bear an extraordinary resemblance to the Etruscan. The transition, as the author of "Eothen" remarks, from this simple form to that of the square, angular pyramid was easy and natural; and the gradations through which the style passed from infancy to its mature enormity can be plainly traced at Sakkara, near Cairo.*

In man's endeavours to make a tomb in a more lasting and permanent form, a monument of large and massive stones suggests itself. Examples of such sepulchral structures composed of gigantic blocks of stone, so as to last through countless ages, and of almost identical forms, have been discovered in many countries, so remotely apart as to preclude all idea of intercommunication.

Cromlechs† and such megalithic structures have almost as wide a range as tumuli. We need not mention those of our own islands as well known. The dolmens of Brittany present gigantic proportions. They are also found in the southern and western departments of France, in Aveiron, Cantal, Tarn, Tarn et Garonne. In Denmark and Sweden they

* Mr. Fergusson also observes that the pyramid must be the lineal descendant of a rude-chambered tumulus or cairn, with external access to the chambers.

† We have adopted the word "cromlech" as more generally in use, though the word "dolmen" is more applicable. Cromlech means in Celtic "crooked stone," from *crom*, crooked or curved; and *lech* a stone. Dolmen is derived from the Celtic word *Daul* a table, and *men* or *maon*, a stone.

L.

frequently occur. M. de Saussure is reported to have found four in Switzerland, and M. de Mortillet has observed a stone circle near Sesto Calende, in Lombardy. Mr. Dennis thus notices those he met at Saturnia, in Etruria. "In the three upright slabs, with their shelving, overlapping lid, we have the exact counterpart of Kit's Coty House, and other like familiar antiquities of Britain, and the resemblances are not only in the form and in the unhewn masses,

No. 51.

KEITLOHEAL STONE CIRCLE—DENMARK.

but even in the dimensions of the structures." There are notices of them in Spain, Portugal, Sardinia, and the Balearic Islands. They occur also in the islands of Malta and Gozo, and in the Canary Islands.

They are found in several parts of India. In the central part of India, in the centre of an immense tract of uncultivated waste, called the Neermul Jungle, where no European ever penetrated, numbers of cromlechs have been found. Dr. Forbes Watson informs us that in the single collectorate of Bellary, there are no fewer than 2,129 cromlechs, kistvaens, &c., and other remains of the so-called pre-historic class, not produced by the aborigines of the country, but by Aryans.

The coast of Malabar also offers an example. Dr. Hooker has called attention to those among the

No. 52.

KIT'S COTY HOUSE.

Khasia people: "Rude stones, he says, of gigantic proportions are erected as monuments, singly, and in rows, circles, or supporting one another like those of Stonehenge, which they resemble in dimensions and appearance." Some have been discovered in the principality of Sorapoor, by Colonel Meadows Taylor, and others have been described by Mr. O'Hara, near Vellore, in the Madras Presidency.*

* According to Colonel Meadows Taylor, the Indian dolmens

148   CROMLECHS AND MEGALITHIC STRUCTURES.

Captain Newbold states, that near Chittore, in North Arcot, he saw a square mile of ground covered with such monuments. In them were found sarco-

INDIAN DOLMEN.

phagi, with the bones of the dead, and pottery of black ware.

are of two kinds—those consisting of four stones, that is to say, three supporting stones and one cap-stone—thus leaving one side open—and those in which the chamber is closed by a fourth stone; in the latter case, this fourth stone has invariably a circular opening in it. This is said to be for the spirit to pass in and out, or to supply food to the departed spirit. As this idea is peculiar to a very low phase of belief, which is still found among some of the lowest African tribes, it shows that the dolmens belong to a very rude and early stage of civilization. Mr. Tylor tells us ("Primitive Culture," p. 409), that the Iroquois also, in old times, used to leave an opening in the grave for the lingering soul to visit its body.

Similar holed stones in cromlechs, evidently for the same purpose, are found in Circassia, in France, and in Cornwall. This is obviously the result of an analogous rude belief common to a low phase of civilization.

Lieut.-Col. W. Ross King mentions the presence on the Nilgiri hills of Druidical circles, cromlechs, kistvaens, and tumuli, precisely similar to those so well known in our own country.

Sir Walter Elliot records their occurrence all over Southern India, from the Nerbudda to Cape Comorin, and probably in Upper India also. Mr. Bruce Foote announces that the Laterite deposits of Madras which he had explored, and in which he had discovered a number of quartzite implements of the drift type, was surmounted in many places by a superficial deposit, containing polished or ground stone implements, and with which were associated stone monuments of the class now under consideration. Colonel Forbes Leslie mentions that stone circles occur in Ceylon surrounding the grave hills.

Lieutenant Oliver has pointed out the resemblance between the megalithic monuments in the Channel Islands, and those in Madagascar, erected at the present day by the hill tribes of Hovas.

In Africa we find evidence of their existence also. Dr. Madden has given a notice of thirteen cromlechs which exist half way between Algiers and Sidi Ferruch, in all important respects identical with our Irish monuments of that name.

Mr. Henry Christy discovered an extensive range

of similar monuments near the sources of the Bournar-mook, near Constantine. "Within an area of more than nine miles, on the mountains as well as on the plains, the whole country around their sources is covered with monuments of the so-called Celtic form, such as dolmens, demi-dolmens, cromlechs, menhirs, alleys, and tumuli ; in a word, there exist there almost all the types known in Europe." Mr. Catherwood has also met with them in the regency of Tunis. The three sites on which we found them were—Sidi Boosi, to the north-east of Hydrah, Welled Agar, and Lhuys. At the first place they were particularly numerous.

Mr. Flower has described cromlechs at Am Gueber El Kalaa Tarf, in his paper on the "Pre-historic Sepulchres of Algeria."

Barth discovered megalithic monuments resembling Stonehenge in character, in the neighbourhood of Tripoli; he also discovered stone circles as low down as the neighbourhood of Mourzouk.

Dr. Bell gives a drawing of some among the mountains of the Caucasus.

At Darab, to the eastward of the province of Fars, in Persia, stone circles have been discovered. To the south of the Caspian sea, between Tauris and Casbin, Chardin also noticed large stone circles in 1672.

On the banks of the Jordan, Captains Irby and

Mangles observed some very singular interesting, and certainly very ancient, tombs, composed of rough stones, resembling what is called Kit's Coty House; and many have been lately discovered in Palestine, by the Exploration Committee. In Moab, De Saulcy observed rude stone avenues and other monuments, which he compares to Celtic dolmens; and Dr. Stanley saw, a few miles to the north of Tyre, a circle of rough upright stones.

Captain Wilson records the existence of circles, similar to our "Druid's circle," being decidedly sepulchral in character, in the peninsula of Sinai.

In the central part of Arabia, in Kaseem, Mr. Palgrave met with similar structures. He says:—
"We saw before us several huge stones, like enormous boulders, placed endways perpendicularly on the soil, while some of them yet upheld similar masses laid transversely over the summit; they were arranged in a curve, and forming part, it would appear, of a large circle, and many other fragments lay rolled on the ground at a moderate distance,—the number of those still upright, was, to speak by memory, eight or nine. Two, at about ten or twelve feet apart one from the other, and resembling huge gate-posts, yet bore their horizontal lintel, a long block laid across them. Pointing towards Rass, our companions affirmed that

a second and similar stone circle, also of gigantic dimensions, existed there." Mr. Palgrave remarks "that there was little difference between the stone wonder of Kaseem, and that of Somersetshire, except the one is in Arabia, and the other, though the more perfect, in England." Koben, a Jewish missionary, is said to have discovered recently three stone circles in Arabia, near Khabb, in the district of Kaseem, evidently the same noticed by Mr. Palgrave, and which are described as being extremely like Stonehenge, and consisting of very lofty triliths.

Mr. Lamont, in his "Wild Life among the Pacific Islanders," describes a stone circle in one of the Penrhyn Islands. "He reached," he says, "an open space of some hundred yards square. It was encircled by tall flat stones, some six feet in height, though generally much lower, but not more than a few inches in thickness—a sort of Stonehenge in a small way. Through the open spaces he could observe several more stones of the same kind, some lying horizontally, supported by others, not unlike the cromlechs of Ireland, but more regular in form, and evidently intended for tombs."

Stone circles have been also noticed by T. H. Hood, in his notes of a cruise in H.M.S. *Fawn*, in Strong's Island, Paadsen, Easter Island, and Waibu.

The Rev. J. Wood* describes a megalithic tomb in one of the Tonga Islands. "All great families bury their dead in a solid vault, about eight feet long by six wide, and eight deep. It is made of five enormous stones, the upper one, which forms the cover, being necessarily larger than the others." At a burial he describes, it took nearly two hundred men to raise the stone cover.

Even in Australia stone circles are said to occur. Mr. Ormond, in a letter to Sir J. V. Simpson, says that he has seen many near the Mount Elephant Plains, in Victoria. They are "from 10 to 100 feet in diameter, and sometimes there is an inner circle. The stones composing these circles, or circular areas, vary in size and shape. Human bones have been dug out of mounds near these circles. The aborigines have no traditions respecting them. When asked about them, they invariably deny knowledge of their origin."

Mr. J. Wood, in his "Natural History of Man,"† notices also their occurrence in Australia. "The blacks," he says, "of Clarence river, place a number of stones in a circle, and in the centre they erect an upright slab of stone. They give no reason for this custom, but only say that 'black fellu make it so,' or 'it belong to black fella.' The former reply signifies

* "Natural History of Man," p. 334.   † Page 68.

that the custom has always prevailed among the nations, and the second that the tomb shows that a native is buried beneath the upright stone."

The most important discovery of these megalithic monuments has been made in Peru, by Mr. Squier. He thus describes them: "There is a class of stone structures in Peru belonging to what is regarded through the world as the earliest monumental period, coincident in style and character with the cromlechs, dolmens, and 'Sun' or 'Druidical' circles, so called of Scandinavia, the British Islands, France, and Northern and Central Asia. The first and simplest form of the burial monument, and which I shall assume, for the present, to be the oldest, consists of flat, unhewn stones of varying lengths, set firmly in the ground, projecting above it from one to two feet, so as to form a circle, more or less regular, about three feet in diameter. The body was buried within this circle, in a sitting or crouching posture, and with a vase of pottery or some other utensil or implement at its feet. Sometimes a few flat stones were laid across the upright ones, so as to form a kind of roof; and, in a few instances, these rude tombs were placed side by side in long rows, and stones afterwards heaped over them, so as to give them the appearance of lines of ruined walls.

CROMLECHS AND MEGALITHIC STRUCTURES. 155

"Another rude but more advanced and impressive form of the tomb, consists of large slabs of stone, projecting from four to six feet above the ground, and also set in the form of a circle or square, of from six to sixteen feet in diameter; these uprights support blocks of stone, which lap over each other inwardly, until they touch, and brace against each other, thus forming a kind of rude arch. A doorway or opening is often found leading into the vault, formed by

PRIMITIVE TOMB—ACORA, PERU.—FROM SQUIER.

omitting one of the upright stones. The arid plain to the south of the town of Acora, near the shores of Lake Titicaca, and twelve miles distant from the ancient town of Chucuito, is covered with remains of this kind, of which Fig. 54 is an example."

"The celebrated ruins," he says, "of Tiahuanaco, in Bolivia, which may be called the Stonehenge or Carnac of the new world, afford a striking example of the artificial arrangement of rough as well as upright stones, in the form of squares and rectangles, and on parallel lines. The megalithic remains of Tiahuanaco rank second in interest to none in the world."

Mr. Squier also notices the stone circles found in Peru. "In many places," he says, "we discover circles defined by rude, upright stones, and surrounding

No. 55.

INTIHUANAS (SUN CIRCLES) OF SILLUSTANI, PERU.—FROM SQUIER.

one or more larger upright stones, placed sometimes in the centre of the circle, but oftener at one-third of the diameter of the circle apart, and on a line at right angles to another line that might be drawn through the centre of the gateway, or entrance on the east. Some of these circles are more elaborate than others, as shown in the engraving (Fig. 55), from which it will be seen that while the one nearest the spectator is constructed of simple upright stones, set in the ground; the second one is surrounded by a platform of stones more or less hewn and fitted together.* The first circle is about ninety feet in diameter; the second about one hundred and fifty feet, and has a single erect stone standing in the relative position he had already indicated. A remarkable feature in the larger circle is a groove cut in the platform around it, deep enough to receive a ship's cable." He concludes his description by again remarking "the close resemblance, if not absolute identity, of the primitive monuments of the great Andean plateau, elevated thirteen thousand feet above the sea, and fenced in with high mountains and frigid deserts, with those of the other continent."

Mr. Squier gives a notice of another stone circle in New Grenada. In his "Antiquities of New York," he introduces an account given in a letter from Signor Velez, of the discovery of monuments, in the province of Tunja, New Grenada, which, as he says, exhibit a close relationship to the primitive stone circles, and

* Mr. Fergusson is inclined to suppose that these are the foundation courses of a circular building, the upper parts of which have perished. The cromlech with stone circle at Tarf, Algeria (see Plate V., fig. 8), presenting an analogous course of flat stones, will suggest that there can be no foundation for this view.

other analogous structures of the old continent. The following is an extract from Signor Velez's letter: "After traversing the province of Leiva in different directions, and after advancing as far as the neighbourhood of Moniquiva, by following the route from Gachantiva to this place, across a beautiful gently sloping plain under cultivation, I discovered a large stone, which, seen some distance off, did not at first appear as if wrought by the hand of man. On approaching it, I found it was a sort of column, 4½ varas in length, by 3½ in diameter. It seemed to me that such stones, although rudely wrought, must have served as columns. On examining the locality, I found, scattered here and there, other stones similar to the first, and at last thirteen stones, of the largest size, ranged as in a circle, about fifty varas in circumference."

That all those megalithic structures were exclusively sepulchral does not now admit of doubt. Skeletons have been frequently found in the cromlechs of Brittany, the Channel Islands, and in Denmark. Excavations made in those of other countries have almost all yielded evidences of their being places of sepulture. As Mr. Fergusson remarks in his recent work on "Rude Stone Monuments," page 509, "Honour to the dead, and propitiation of the spirits of the departed, seem to have been the two leading ideas that, both in the East and West, gave rise to the erection of these hitherto mysterious structures which are found numerously scattered over the face of the old world."

The author of an article in the "Edinburgh Review," on non-historic times, suggests a very reasonable classification of this class of sepulchral monuments: "It may probably be assumed," he says, "that the dolmen or cromlech was originally a stone cist in the centre of a tumulus, meant to contain either one or more bodies. This, afterwards, was expanded into a chamber for the accommodation of several. In the third stage it was furnished with a passage or avenue of entrance, so as to be permanently accessible. In the fourth stage, the covering tumulus was dispensed with; but the last form most probably was when the cromlech was placed externally on the top of the mound as a mere ornament or simulated tomb; as we find in France and Algiers.*

It can be also proved that stone circles were, too, almost exclusively sepulchral, while, as the same writer quoted remarks, " It is not difficult to trace their progressive development. They were first an enclosure

* The cromlech at Tarf, in Algoria, has a sepulchral chamber under it; it must have been, therefore, a simulated tomb.

or temenos around tumuli.* When dolmens or cromlechs came to be external they are found surrounding them as they did the tumuli; and lastly, when the use of these two classes of monuments was dying out, they came to be used as simple circles without any visible enclosed object. In this last form they are found principally in Great Britain and the Danish Isles. There are not less than two hundred circles of various sizes in these islands. One hundred of these, at least, when examined have yielded sepulchral deposits." Mr. John Stuart who is certainly one of the best informed antiquaries living, has come to the same conclusion with regard to those of Scotland and England. He writes: "The result of various systematic excavations of 'standing stones,' both single and in groups, goes to establish that, in almost every case, the stone circles, which have for a time received the unfortunate name of 'Druidical Temples' are really places of sepulture."†

* With all due deference to the writer, I would suggest that an enclosure round a single upright stone, under which the body was buried, as we see at Jewurgi, in India, in Algeria, and in Australia, was the first stage. In Plate V., I have traced the sequence and progressive development of the stone circle from the earliest rude circular enclosure of stones, round an upright one, till it culminates in Stonehenge.

† Mr. John Stuart in his paper on "Stone Circles," in the transactions of the International Congress of Pre-historic Archæ-

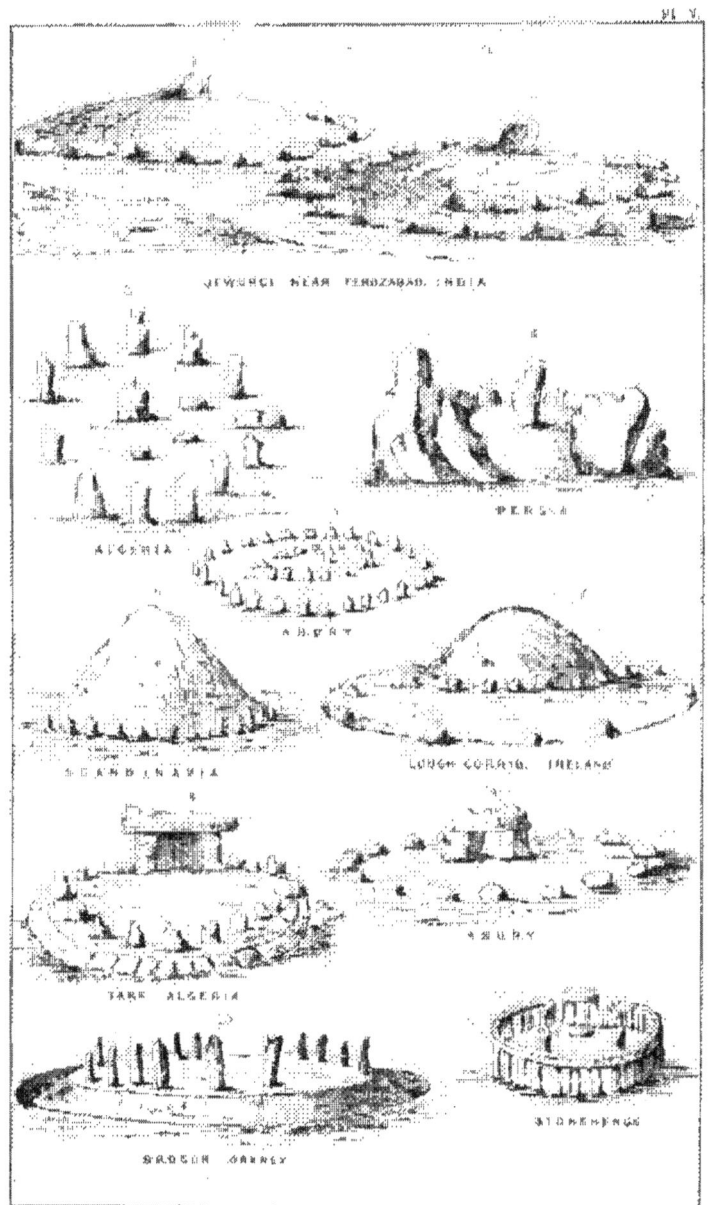

The *alignments* or *avenues* of upright stones form another class of these megalithic monuments. When attached to circles, as the same author suggests, it is not difficult to see that they are only hypæthral copies of the passages which lead to the sepulchral chambers or tumuli. In this form they are found on Dartmoor, in Cumberland; and as Mr. Stuart remarks, "If the cairns at New Grange were removed, the pillars would form another Callernish."

ology, gives the following propositions as deduced from facts and authorities, contained in a memoir in the second volume of the "Sculptured Stones of Scotland."

15. The theory which ascribes to stone circles the purpose of temples or courts is modern, and unsupported by facts.

16. No early author speaks of circles as temples or courts. In early records, they are frequently referred to as the "standing stones" (Lapides stantes); or, as at Stennis, in Orkney, "the stones" or at Stonehenge as the "Stone-henges." Some of them are referred to as monuments of the dead, and at times as petrified dancers.

19. In the seventeenth century a theory was proposed by two English writers, John Aubrey and William Stukely, which ascribed the great circles of Stonehenge and Avebury to the Druids as their temples; and since their day all stone circles have been called "Druidical circles."

20. This theory rests on no authority of facts, observation, or analogy.

21. The Druids described by Cæsar and other classical writers, are never mentioned in connection with stone circles.

22. These Druids were local in their occurrence, while stone circles are found throughout Europe, Africa, and Asia, and we may now add America.

There is also another class of monuments which have been named *menhirs*, tall or long stones, or peulvens, as the French sometimes call them. They have a very wide range. They seem to be of all ages, and used for all purposes. The earliest mention of them in writing is in the Bible, Genesis xxxi., and in Exodus xxiv. 4, and in Joshua iv. 21, 22. In all these instances they were memorial stones, but they are also frequently found marking graves. They are sometimes *cat* stones or memorials of battles, and certainly were sometimes used as boundary stones.

The sepulchral circle of Stonehenge is only a further development on a more extensive and grander scale of the rude cromlech and circle, as the pyramid is of the simple mound. In Stonehenge we find combined the stone circle and the cromlech. We have the circular plan of the original stone enclosure, and the arrangement of the large stone of the cromlech placed horizontally over the side stones in the trilithon.* That Stonehenge was a place of

* This view is confirmed by the high authority of Mr. Fergusson. His impression is ("Rude Stone Monuments," p. 100), that the trilithon is only an improved dolmen, standing on two legs instead of three or four. The trilithon seems to have been a sepulchral form adopted also in many other countries. Olaus Magnus describes the most honourable monuments of the great of his country as erected with immense stones, and formed like great gates or trilithons. Other trilithons occur also near St. Nazaire

CROMLECHS AND MEGALITHIC STRUCTURES. 163

burial and not a temple is proved by analogy, as the large stone circles of Khasin, Algiers, as well as the smaller ones of the British Isles, Denmark, the Penrhyn Islands, and Australia, are all sepulchral. Further it is admitted by antiquarians, that early and primitive races never erected temples. It is supposed they were, in many respects, like the American Indians; they recognised a great spirit, but had no representations of him, and had no temples. They seem to have had scarcely any religious observances, still less any edifices for sacred purposes. Temples argue an advanced civilization. The Jews had no temple until the time of Solomon. To erect such a structure as Stonehenge for a temple would argue a more advanced stage of civilization than could have existed in England at the period in which it was built, which was evidently at the close of the stone age. To erect a temple, people should

in France, at Ksaca, and Elkub in Tripoli, and in Arabia as described by Mr. Palgrave. Lieut. Meade ("Ride through New Zealand," p. 300), describes a trilithon in Tongatabu, which is evidently sepulchral. "It consists," he says, "of two perpendicular blocks of stone, about twenty-five or thirty feet high, supporting a horizontal one about half as long again. In the centre of the latter is a circular hollow or basin, which the natives call the gods, or giants, 'Kava-bowl.'"

Mr. Fergusson ("Stone Monuments," p. 100), gives an illustration of a trilithon, in Syria, of a Roman period.

M 2

have some material object of worship, some visible form; and the ancient Britons who were in that rude phase of civilization peculiar to the stone age, had none.

To further confirm our view, that Stonehenge was solely a place of sepulture, we shall quote the high authorities of Mr. John Stuart, Sir James Simpson, and Mr. Fergusson, who have adduced the most convincing reasons. Mr. John Stuart writes: "If we must recognize the smaller stone circles to be ancient sepulchres, I think it is reasonable that we should regard the larger examples as of the same kind, but of greater importance. Such structures as Stonehenge and Stennis, may have resulted from some great national effort to commemorate mighty chiefs. The royal mausoleum of our day differs more in character from the humble headstone, and the great mound at Kertch from a common grave, than does Stonehenge from the circle at Crichie, although all have a common origin. The remains of most ancient people attest that greater and more enduring labour and art have been expended on the construction of tombs for the dead than in abodes for the living."

Sir James Simpson gives it as his opinion, that "We have not a particle of direct evidence for the too common belief that our stone circles were temples which the Druids use for worship, or that our cromlechs were their sacrificial altars."

Mr. Fergusson writes: "We have in the British Isles at least one hundred circles with or without dolmens in the centre, similar in all essential respects with the inner circles at Avebury, and all of which on being dug into have proved to be sepulchral. On the other hand, not one single circle has been proved to have been ever erected for or used as a temple; and not one plausible suggestion has been made either as to the deities to whom they were dedicated, or the form of worship which could be performed in them. In almost every other country of the world, savage or civilized, the temples of the gods are improved, enlarged, and beautified repetitions of dwellings or halls of the living, erected at leisure, and ornamented from time to time with all the best skill the nation can afford, and are generally proportioned to the wants of the community. It seems inconceivable that a few shepherds scattered over the Wiltshire downs could have required a temple five times the area of St. Peter's at Rome."

A striking feature in the comparison of the various accounts of these megalithic structures, wherever met with over the world, is more than the analogy between them, the almost identity of form among them all. There are, indeed, some small peculiarities and differences in these megalithic structures in different countries, but the same principle, the same simple form has been evolved and carried out independently.

Another feature, which is very striking, is the gigantic scale on which these structures were raised. It would appear as if nations in their earliest periods were more active, produced more wonderful works, and executed structures which outvie in rude magnitude the boldest efforts of modern genius; as instances, we can mention the circle of Stonehenge, the stone avenues of Carnac, and the Cyclopean galleries of Tiryns. When we recollect that these were the first efforts of the human race, made without pattern, designed without exemplar, commenced and carried out without experience, they cannot but give us a high idea of the energy and skill of man in the earlier stage of his development. As Dr. Wilson observes, "There seems to be an epoch in the early history of man, when what may be styled the megalithic era of art developes itself under the utmost variety of circumstances. It is one of the most characteristic features pertaining to the development of human thought in the earliest stages of constructive skill."

Judging from the various accounts of the state of civilization in connection with the builders of these megalithic structures, they were in a very rude and barbarous phase. Dr. Hooker informs us that the Khasias, among whom these cromlechs are built even at the present day, are a barbarous and savage people. He describes them as a race of a most bloodthirsty disposition, and who fight with bows and arrows. Human sacrifices and polyandry are said to be frequent among them, and their orgies are detestable. As among all rude races, some are tattooed. They are superstitious, but have no religion. Their method of removing the blocks for their dolmens and menhirs is by cutting grooves, along which fires are lighted, and into which, when heated, cold water is run, which causes the rock to fissure along the groove. The blocks are erected by dint of sheer brute force, the lever being the only aid.

The hill tribes of Hovas, a rude people in Madagascar, Lieutenant Oliver informs us, also erect megalithic structures at the present day.

Now we may reasonably infer that the early Britons, Danes, and Irish, who erected cromlechs, were in a similar and analogous phase, and adopted similar means for erecting their structures. We have on historic record, that the Britons had attained a low degree of civilization at the time the Romans became acquainted with them; their clothing was skins, and they were in the habit of staining and tattooing their bodies. Cæsar, in speaking of the Britons of his age, says they stained themselves with woad, which makes them of a blue tinge, and gives them a more fearful appearance in battle. Every ten or twelve of them had their wives in common. They were much addicted to superstitious observances, and human sacrifices were frequent. The Celts of Brittany, where cromlechs so frequently occur, were in a similar rude and savage phase at the time of Cæsar.

The early Irish, according to Diodorus Siculus and Strabo, were cannibals. From the numbers of rude flint and stone implements, and the bones of wild animals in connection with them, found wide-spread all over Ireland, the natural inference is, that the primitive Irish must have been in a very rude and barbarous state, living entirely by the chase or by fishing.

Professor Nilsson has shown that the sepulchres of Denmark and Sweden, which were erected of large stones collected together by main force, are of the stone age, when the peoples of those countries were in a rude and uncivilized state. "For," he says, "the earliest hunting implements of stone in every country are synchronous with the first appearance of the savage there, since he required at once the flesh of wild animals for food and their skins for clothing."

That these cromlechs were raised during the stone age receives additional confirmation from Sir John Lubbock's observation, when noticing a pile of stonework in the island of Tahiti. "It is perhaps," he says, "the most important monument which is known to have been constructed with *stone tools only*, and renders it the less unlikely that some of the large tumuli and other ancient monuments of Europe may belong to the stone age;" and the Tahitians of that age, it is well known, were in a very barbarous state.

In India there is a tradition with regard to the cromlechs there, "that the stones were put up by a people who lived in the country before Buddhism or Brahminism was introduced." Mr. Capper, in his work on India, says, "There seems to be little doubt but that, at one period, the Deccan (the part of India where most cromlechs are found) was peopled by others than Hindoos. The aborigines are said to have been foresters and mountaineers, leading a wild and lawless life; but this must have been at a very remote period, for there is abundance of proof that an advanced state of civilization prevailed previous to the time of the Greek notices of India."

Professor Huxley also confirms this, as he describes the inhabitants of the Deccan as a primitive people, speaking languages (termed Dravidian) entirely different from those of the Aryan race, and differing also in their customs, having no Brahmins or castes, but eating flesh of all kinds, worshipping their ancestors, permitting polyandry, and not burning widows." He also observes, that in these non-Aryan districts are found remarkable monuments; raised masses of stone, one perched on another, forming chambers or tumuli, which contain human burnt bones, spear-heads, and the remains of food; and thus very closely resembling the cromlechs or dolmens found especially in Cornwall, Brittany, and throughout Western Europe. He further remarks the analogies existing between the Deccan people and the Australian, whom he characterizes as savages of the lowest condition.

Lieut.-Colonel W. Ross King tells us that the Todas, a wild and rude tribe of the Nilgiri mountains, at the present day, invariably burn the remains of their dead within a circle of stones, and afterwards bury them there.

These megalithic monuments are not, however,

confined solely to the non-Aryan races, for Mr. Forbes Watson tells us that the cromlechs in Bellari were raised, not by the aborigines, but by Aryans. As Mr. Charnock very justly remarks, "The so-called Druidical remains in India, and elsewhere, might be the work of any people."

In Australia, the Penrhyn Islands, and other islands of the Pacific Ocean, and also among the Hovas of Madagascar, where stone circles and megalithic structures occur, the people are in the lowest state of barbarism. We may, therefore, come to this conclusion in regard to these megalithic structures, that they are not peculiar to the Celtic, Scythian, or any other people, but are the result of an endeavour to secure a lasting and permanent place of sepulture among a people in a rude and primitive phase of civilization; and that they were raised by men who were led by a natural instinct to build them in the simplest, and consequently the almost identical, form in all countries.*

* The strongest proof of the style of those megalithic structures not being derived from another country by migration, and of their independent development, is the progressive style of these monuments in each country where they are found. They exhibit in England, Ireland, Denmark, Brittany, Algiers, and India, a sequence and a progress, beginning from the simplest and rudest form up to the most complete and perfected style. [Mr.

We have shown that they occur in countries—Syria, India, Africa, Peru, the Penrhyn Islands, Madagascar, and Australia—where neither Celts nor Scythians ever put their foot.

We shall now conclude by extracting the following eloquent passage from Mr. Dennis' "Cemeteries of Etruria." "This form of sepulchre (the cromlech) can hardly be indicative of any race in particular. The structure is so rude and simple that it might have suggested itself to any people, and be naturally adopted in an early state of civilization. It is the very arrangement the child makes use of in building his house of cards. This simplicity accounts for the wide diffusion of such monuments over the old world, for they are found in different climates and widely

---

Mr. Lukis remarks, with regard to the Dolmens in Brittany: "Their forms are very varied; and these forms indicate not merely a long residence of their builders in this country, but, as I believe, a progress in constructive science."

Mr. Squier is convinced when speaking of the megalithic monuments of Peru, "That there has been a gradual development of these rude remains into elaborate and imposing monuments, corresponding with them in their purpose and design, or a gradual change from the rough burial chamber of uncut stones into the symmetrical tower built of hewn blocks accurately fitted together, and that we may reasonably infer that the latter were constructed by the same people that built the first, and that, monumentally at least, the civilization of Peru was indigenous, gradually developed, and not intruded."

distant countries, from the mountains of Wales and Ireland to the deserts of Barbary, and from the western shores of the Iberian peninsula to the steppes of Tartary and the eastern coasts of Hindostan. They are found on mountains and in plains, on continents and in islands, on the sea coast and far inland, by the river and in the desert, solitary and grouped in multitudes. That, in certain instances, they may be of the same people, in different countries, is not to be gainsaid; but there is no necessity to seek for one particular race as the constructors of these monuments, or even as the originators of the type."

We may add also the words of Mr. Squier, who, in his "Primeval Monuments of Peru," gives it as his matured opinion "that there exist in Peru and Bolivia, high up among the snowy Andes, the oldest forms of monuments, sepulchral or otherwise, known to mankind, exact counterparts in character of those of the 'old world,' having a common design illustrating similar conceptions, and all of them the work of the same peoples found in occupation of the country at the time of the Conquest, and whose later monuments are mainly, if not wholly, the developed forms of those raised by their ancestors, and which seem to have been *the spontaneous productions of the primitive* *man* in all parts of the world, and *not necessarily, nor even probably derivative*."*

* Mr. John Evans adopts the same view. His words are: "The curious similarity observed among megalithic monuments in different parts of the world may possibly be due to some analogous development of thought and feeling, rather than to any intimate connection between the races who erected them. The Dolmens of Algeria, described by Mr. Flowers, those of Brittany by Mr. Lukis, those of the Aveyron by Mr. Cartailhac, are all, more or less, closely allied to the ancient sepulchres and Panderkulis of the Nilgiri Mountains in Southern India, described by Sir Walter Elliot."—*Review of the Transactions of the International Congress of Pre-historic Archæology in "Nature."*

NOTE.—In further confirmation of the view taken in this chapter, that under similar circumstances man will do the same thing in the same way or nearly so, I can mention the lake dwellings discovered in widely apart and unconnected countries. We have in these dwellings, instances of a people at an early period living in a state of insecurity on the borders of a lake, when the thought was naturally suggested to them that, by driving piles, making an island, or by erecting platforms, at a short distance from the shore, they would obtain security from any sudden attack of their enemies. Thus the same thought of adopting identical means, or nearly so, suggested itself independently to the Irishman in his loughs; to the Swiss and Italian in his lakes; to the Papuan on his marshy shores; and to the African in his lagoons. Indeed the similarity has been so great, that in Sir Charles Lyell's "Antiquity of Man," the restoration of the Swiss Lake Dwelling is from a sketch of a similar habitation in New Guinea. In Herodotus we find an historical record of these habitations at an early period, in the mountain lake of Prasias, erected by the Pœonians, and evidently in the same manner for purposes of security; and how justly they depended on them for security may be inferred from the fact that Megabyzus, the general of Darius, was unable to subdue them. We find also another passage of Herodotus, in which he states that Amysis, king of Egypt, in order to escape from the Ethiopians who invaded his kingdom, made himself an island by a mixture of earth and ashes (a crannog), in a corner of the lake of Buto—now Lake Boorloe. (Herod. ii. 140.) Thus we may see that similar circumstances will evolve similar contrivances and expedients.

A similar inference may be drawn with regard to the shell mounds, or kitchen-middens, which occur in various parts of the world. These are refuse heaps of shells, the fish of which had been eaten by the savage tribes living along the sea coast, and then thrown away. Darwin thus describes this custom among the inhabitants of Tierra del Fuego. "The inhabitants, living chiefly upon shell-fish, are obliged constantly to change their place of residence; but they return at intervals to the same spots, as is evident from the pile of old shells, which must often amount to some tons in weight." A like custom has given origin to similar shell heaps in different countries. They are numerous in Denmark. They occur on the Scotch, English, and Irish coasts. One of these accumulations of shells has been found by Sir J. Lubbock at the mouth of the Somme. They are found along the coast of the United States, in East Florida, Georgia, and in Newfoundland. Examples are also met with in South America, at Guazal, Ecuador. Similar remains have been observed by travellers in various parts of the world. In Australia, by Dampier; in Tierra del Fuego, by Darwin; in the Malay peninsula, by Mr. Earle; and at Smyrna, by Mr. Hyde Clarke.

ON ROCK CARVINGS.

THE presence of carvings of rude designs on rocks, stones, monoliths, cromlechs, and other megalithic structures in many countries, bearing a remarkable analogy and likeness to one another, has justly excited much wonder and speculation. They have engaged the attention of many writers, who have published illustrations of them, and have put forward various theories with regard to their origin.

Sir James Simpson has published a very careful and accurate account of the sculpturing of cups and concentric rings on rocks, in various parts of Scotland, accompanied by excellent illustrations. Mr. Tate has published those discovered carved on rocks in Northumberland. Mr. du Noyer has also written some interesting papers on the rock carvings found in Ireland, and Mr. Conwell has given notices of those which occur on the stones at Lough Crew.

We have also accounts of analogous carvings in other parts of the world. In Brittany, the blocks used in the construction of the gallery and chamber of the sepulchral mound at Gavr Inis, in the Morbihan, are densely covered with continuous circular, spiral, zigzag, looped, and various other types of carving. The stones of the tumuli and cromlech at Locmariaker

No. 56.

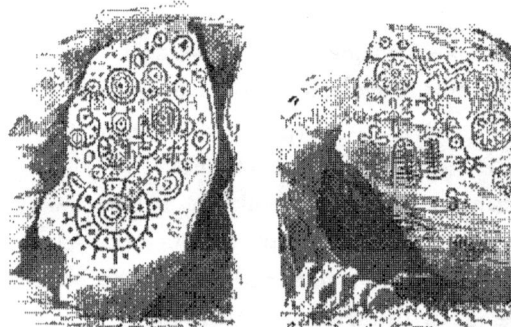

CARVED STONES IN CAIRN—LOUGH CREW.

present figures of various military weapons and arms, with some imperfect figures of animals.

Analogous carvings of circles, and very rude sketches of canoes and rowers, have been found on rocks and cromlechs in Scandinavia.

Rude representations of animals, with inscriptions, occur on rocks near Mount Sinai, which have been attributed to wandering pastoral tribes.

In almost every part of North America, in the most secluded and least populated districts, where there are no other evidences that man ever existed, rude sculptures on rocks and cliffs are found. The sculptured rock in Forsyth Co. Georgia, presents concentric circles almost identical with those of Northumberland,* and Lough Crew in Ireland.

Humboldt mentions " rocks covered with sculptured figures " in several parts of South America. He thus

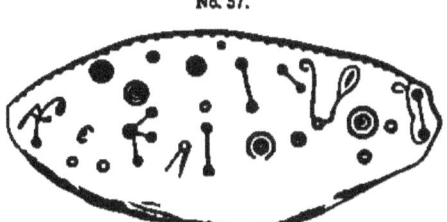

No. 57.

SCULPTURED ROCK—FORSYTH CO. GEORGIA.

notices some on the Orinoco: " We were shown, near the rock Culimacasi, on the banks of the Cassiquiare, and at the port of Caycara, in the lower Orinoco, traces which were believed to be regular characters.

* Dr. Griffiths stated at the Machynlleth meeting that Queen Emma of the Sandwich Islands, on being shown by him some of these markings (on stones), stated that others existed, identically the same in her own island, and of which the natives gave an amusing and ingenious explanation. —*Archæologia Cambrensis*, 3rd series, l. p. 156.

They were, however, only misshapen figures representing the heavenly bodies, together with tigers, crocodiles, boas, and instruments used for making the flour of cassava. It was impossible to recognise on these painted rocks ('piedras pintadas,' the name by which the natives denote those masses loaded with figures) any symmetrical arrangement, or characters with regular spaces."

Mr. Squier has discovered carved rocks at Masaya, in Nicaragua. "These carvings," he says, "covered the face of the cliffs for more than a hundred yards, and consisted chiefly of rude representations of animals and men, with some ornamented, and perhaps arbitrary figures, the significance of which is unknown." He adds that rocks, inscribed in very much the same manner, are scattered all over the continent, from the shores of New England to Patagonia. Most, if not all of them, are the work of savage tribes.

Mr. Bollaert describes an engraved stone found at Caldera, Western Veraguas, as a granite block, known to the country people as the "piedra pintada," or painted stone. It is fifteen feet high, nearly fifty feet in circumference, and flat at the top. Every part, especially the eastern side, is covered with figures. One represents a radiant sun; it is followed by a series of heads, all with some variation, scorpions, and fantastic figures. The top and the other sides have signs of a circular and oval form, crossed by lines. The sculpture is ascribed to the Dorachos, a numerous tribe, which formerly inhabited those parts. Several other monuments, tombs of the same tribe, are mentioned as being covered with fantastic figures, or representations of natural objects.

Other rocks, or piedras pintadas, are mentioned by the same author as representing figures of animals, branches of flowers, and other strange characters of various angles. One in particular is described, not far from Quito: "In this solitary spot (the ravine of the sun), shaded by luxuriant vegetation, rises an insulated mass of sandstone. On the surface of the rock are concentric circles, representing the image of the sun." This rock is thus described by Humboldt: "One of the surfaces of this small rock is remarkable for its whiteness; it is cut perpendicularly, as if it had been worked by the hand of man. On this smooth and white ground are concentric circles, which represent the image of the sun, such as at the commencement of civilization we see figured among every nation of the earth. These circles are of a blackish-brown, and, in the space they enclose, we perceive some lines half effaced, which indicate two eyes and a mouth. On a close examination of the rock, we discovered that the concentric circles were small veins of brown iron ore, very common in every formation of sandstone; the lines which indicate the eyes and the mouth are evidently traced by means of some metallic tool."*

Others are described by Mr. Bollaert in the valley of the Pintadas, at the foot of the Andes, consisting

* Basalt, also, when the decomposition of the rock has not been considerable, exhibits a concentric arrangement of coats round centres at variable distances from each other. The early men being, like children, fond of imitation, may have copied these concentric circles of natural formation. Sir James Simpson has pointed out, that "All the cup-like excavations which we meet with on megalithic circles, monoliths, &c., are not by any means the work of man. Many of them are, on the contrary, the work of nature; or, in other words, the results of the weathering and disintegration of the stone from long exposure. Among the endless vagaries of shape and form effected on rocks by weathering, cup-like excavations occur frequently on the surfaces of primary sandstone, and other softer rocks, like those of the Semdio stones in Fife, and the Duddo circle in Northumberland. The surface of the Carline Stone, near Dunmore House, presents a series of smooth, cup-like excavations; but they are all the result of round included masses, having been weathered out of the amygdaloid rock of which the stone is composed." Some of the concentric circles figured on the stones in Northumberland may be the rude representation of the circular labyrinth, which occurs on the reverse of the coins of Gnossus in Crete, and may have been introduced by the Greek missionaries, who spread over all the north of Europe in the early centuries of the church. Mr. Stuart regards all the cave sculptures in Scotland as the work of these early missionaries.

of representations of Indians, llamas, dogs, and other forms, on the side of the desert ravine, some of the figures being thirty feet or more in height, cut or rather scraped out in the sandy soil, the lines being twelve to eighteen inches broad, and six inches deep.

At one league from Macaya he observed a large isolated block, twelve feet square, called the Piedra del Leon, covered with very old Indian sculptures. The centre group consists of a man wrestling with a puma; also figures of llamas, guanacos, circles, serpents, &c. These figures are not chiselled, but picked out with some pointed instrument. He supposes it to be a very ancient Aymara work. Mr. Bollaert was informed that at Mani, to the south of Peru, there were sculptured stones with the sun, moon, and stars, Indians, and animals.

A granite rock, eight leagues north of Arequipa, Peru, presents rude representations of the human figure and of animals, with the usual circles enclosing a cross.

Mr. Brett has discovered carved rocks presenting some curious configurations on the river Corentyn, in Guiana, drawings of which we give from Mr. Brett's "Guiana."

In Australia, at the head of Sydney harbour, rude and ancient figures of the kangaroo have been found

TIMEHRI OR CARVED ROCKS ON THE RIVER CORENTYN
(Sketched by Capt Allen)

sculptured on the rocks. In a cave on the north-eastern coast, Mr. Cunningham observed certain "tolerable figures of sharks, porpoises, turtles, lizards, trepang, starfish, clubs, canoes, water-gourds, and some quadrupeds, which were probably intended to represent kangaroos and dogs." The natives round Sydney also frequently drew upon the rocks " various figures of fish, clubs, swords, animals, and branches of trees, not contemptibly represented."

The Rev. J. C. Wood, in his " Natural History of Man," page 95, gives a description of many rock carvings discovered in Australia by Mr. Angus. " He found," Mr. Angus says, " all the most out of the way and the least accessible headlands adorned with carvings, and also that the whole of the subjects represented *indigenous* objects, such as kangaroos, opossums, sharks, the heileman, or shield, the boomerang, and, above all, the human figure in the attitudes of the Corroboree dances." He adds: "An old writer on New South Wales, about the year 1803, remarks, when referring to the natives; ' they have some taste for sculpture, most of their instruments being carved with rude work, effected with pieces of broken shell; and on the rocks are frequently to be seen various figures of fish, clubs, swords, animals, &c., not contemptibly represented.'"

At the Cape, the Bushmen, one of the rudest existing races of humanity, live much in caves, and frequently paint on the walls of them the animals of the neighbourhood, and sometimes battle and hunting scenes, always in profile.

Mr. Christy also mentions some Bushmen paintings found in caverns, and on flat stone surfaces near some of their permanent water supplies. One side of one of the caverns was covered with outlines of animals, only the upper part was distinguishable, and evidently represented the wilde beest, or gnoo, the koodoo, quagga, &c.

In the Fifeshire caves, sculptured representations of the horse, the dog, the bear, the deer, fish, serpents, also the comb and mirror, almost identical with those found upon the sculptured stones in other parts of Scotland, have been lately discovered.

Similar caves, with sculptured figures, occur in St. Domingo.

Livingstone discovered a large tribe in Rua, in central Africa, living in underground houses. The " writings" therein, he was told by some of the people, were drawings of animals, not letters.

Even in the earliest and rudest ages, man, as Sir James Simpson says, was a " sculpturing and painting animal," and exhibited his love of imitation when his artistic instinct was evolved. Amongst the relics found in the Perigord caves, there have been discovered sculpturings upon stone, bone, and ivory of different animals, and lately, a rude sketch of a mammoth.

Various have been the conjectures with regard to the origin of these carvings and sculpturings, the age at which they were carved, and the race of men who carved them.

Professor Nilsson attributes those found in Scandinavia to a Phœnician origin, and considers the circles as symbols of the sun and the other heavenly bodies —a most untenable hypothesis, as there are no similar carvings among Phœnician remains with which to connect them. Besides this, analogous and identical circles and carvings are found in America, where no Phœnician influence could possibly have reached.

Others suggest that they are symbols or symbolic enumerations of families and tribes, or some variety of archaic writing or philosophical emblems.* But

* The following paragraph extracted from the "Athenæum," affords an instance of the absurdity of those learned theories. "The philological world of Berlin has been much disturbed by rubbings of inscriptions from that mysterious seat of colossal stone figures, Easter Island. These inscriptions, set out in good straight lines, look like the repetition of various alphabetical characters, bearing some of them a striking likeness to later Hebrew, but, unhappily,

from the rudeness of these rock sculpturings, it is evident that the men who carved them must have been in a very low state of civilization, and consequently could not have had any idea of symbolism. Symbolism belongs to a more advanced age, and to more reflective minds. Almost all of these carved figures are evidently merely rude representations of actual objects.

In the opinion of some authors they are designed to commemorate events of greater or less importance, but, as Mr. Squier remarks, of the rock carvings at Macaya, they are for the most part far too rude to be of much value.

We shall, I think, be led to a more just conclusion as to their origin if we bring before our minds that man, in his rude, early, and primitive age, bears a great analogy in his thoughts and actions to a child. The savage and the primitive man have the same fondness for imitation, the same love of industrious

---

undecipherable. The important results to be obtained are, however, no longer in expectation, as Professor Huxley has solved the inscriptions, which might long have puzzled the learned world. He has recognized the rubbings as impressions from moulds used by the Polynesians in printing the patterns on the *tapa* cloth, the ancient dress of Tahiti and other islands. This accounts for the geometrical and regular reproduction of details, which are not ideographs, hieroglyphs, or alphabetic symbols."

idleness, as the child. A child will pass hours whittling and paring a stick, building a diminutive house or wall, and tracing forms on the turf. The savage will wear away years in carving his war club, and polishing his stone adze. As the Rev J. C. Wood observes: "All savages are idle. He may, perhaps, condescend to carve the posts of his house into some fantastical semblance of the human form, or he may, perchance, employ himself in slowly rubbing a stone club into shape, or in polishing or adorning his weapon." These considerations lead me to attribute these carvings and sculptures to the industrious idleness of a pastoral people; passing the long and weary days in tending their flocks and herds, they amused themselves by carving and cutting these various figures of the sun, the moon, or any animals or objects in their neighbourhood, on the rocks near them.

An interesting instance of this practice we have in the story told of the celebrated painter, Giotto, who was a lowly shepherd boy, and who, while his flocks were feeding around, passed his time in drawing on a smooth fragment of rock, with a pointed stone, the figures of his sheep. This attracted the attention of Cimabue the painter, as he was riding by.

The rude outlines of figures, faces, representations of the sun, moon, and animals (according to the country in which they are found; the mammoth among the early and primitive races; the horse, the dog, the bear, in Europe; the camel on the rocks near Mount Sinai; the llama in Peru; the kangaroo in Australia), by primitive men, like the rude attempts at drawing by children, cannot but bear a family resemblance to one another, their utter absence of art being frequently their chief point of relationship.

This view may seem too simple, but it has the sanction of a high authority. Humboldt, when noticing the sculptured rocks in South America, considers the figures represented, instead of being symbolical, rather as the *fruits of the idleness of hunting nations.* As some are inclined to recognise alphabetic characters in these carvings, he observes ("Cordilleras," i. 154.): " We cannot be too careful not to confound what may be the effect of chance, or *idle amusement,* with letters or syllabic characters. Mr. Truter relates that, in the southern extremity of Africa, among the Betjuanas, he saw idle children busy in tracing on a rock, with some sharp instrument, characters which bore the most perfect resemblance with the P and the M of the Roman alphabet; notwithstanding which, these rude tribes were perfectly ignorant of writing." An account in the "Magasin Pittoresque," of 1864, of similar carvings on the cromlechs lately discovered in the north of Africa, near Constantine, affords further confirmation of this view. "We thought at first to have found designs or characters carved on these stones; but, after a more careful examination, we were convinced that they were lines traced by Arab shepherds with the point of a knife or stone. These capricious designs imitate in general the lines of a draught-board, or of a child's game, called 'morel,' and also those cabalistic signs forming triangles, squares, or lozenges, which we see so frequently on the amulets of the natives."

Sir James Simpson's note, at page 107 of his work, also corroborates this view. "Three years ago my friend, Dr. Arthur Mitchell, saw the herring fishermen, *in a day of idleness*, cutting circles with their knives on the face of the rock, without the operators being able to assign any reason for their work, except that others had done it before them."[*]

[*] A friend tells me that when copying some of the rude rock carvings in Scotland, a farmer happening to be near at the time, he asked him if he knew anything about these carvings. "Indeed, I do," was his answer, "they were done by an idle herd-boy, with a rusty nail."

Dodwell ("Travels in Greece") remarked some rude carvings of temples, and other designs on the rocks in the quarries of Pentelicus, which he justly attributed to the stone masons in their idle moments.

Mr. Hamilton ("Wanderings in North Africa") takes a similar view of certain inscriptions on the walls of Tolmeta: "On the stones are many inscriptions, whose irregularity would lead one to the idea that they are of very recent date, or even to fancy them the work of *industrious idlers* bent upon thus immortalizing their names."

In Italy boys often trace a complicated figure, the

No. 58.

centre of which forms a cross, on the walls;* when asked why, they can give no reason, their only purpose being evidently to kill time.

The Sinaitic inscriptions are now known to be only the memorials of travellers writing their names, and greeting the reader, and desiring to be remembered by him who passes by—a practice adopted by the

* An almost identical figure may be seen traced on the walls of a school-room, in a woodcut in Carleton's "Stories of Irish Peasantry," vol. i. p. 324. It was evidently done by some idle boys.

Smiths, Jones, and Robinsons, of the present day, who wish to immortalize themselves. Lepsius remarks, with regard to the position in which these inscriptions are found, "It is easy to perceive, that it is those places, sheltered from the midday sun, which invited passing travellers on the road to Firan, to engrave their names and short mottoes in the soft rock."*

The Count de Vogüé tells us that " the inscriptions of Safa, situated in the desert, two days' journey east of the Jebel Hauran, appear to contain, like the inscriptions of Sinai, nothing but proper names, accompanied by formulæ of souvenirs, or prayers, gross representations of nomadic life, combats, lion hunts, figures of camels, goats, and women."

According to Mr. Squier, the valley in which the Masaya carvings are, is remarkable for its seclusion and gloom, where the rays of the sun seldom reach.

---

* According to Mr. E. H. Palmer ("Desert of the Exodus," p. 190) they are mere scratches on the rock, the work of idle loungers, consisting, for the most part, of mere names, interspersed with rude figures of men and animals. They generally occur, he says, when there is some pleasant shade, or convenient camping-ground close by. In such places they exist in a confused jumble, reminding one forcibly of those spots which Tourist Cockneyism has marked for its own. The instrument used appears to have been a sharp stone, by which they were dotted in. He attributes them to a commercial people, traders, carriers, and settlers in the land.

It thus appears that the valley was used as a retreat by the rude races of that country, from the fervid heat and fierce rays of the sun; and that, in their idle moments, they busied themselves in carving those rude attempts at the representation of men and animals.

Several of the walls of Pompeii, and of the guard-room of the Prætorian cohort on the Palatine hill at Rome, are covered with rude scratchings (graffiti) and writings; and to the present day the same fashion continues on public walls, and in more retired places, all proceeding from the same spirit of idleness. The love of twiddling and doing something in idle moments is natural to man in all ages and climes. This is as common a peculiarity of the Irishman, who cuts and hacks his stick as he tramps along the road, as of the savage Indian, who, when he retreats under the shadow of a tree or a rock, in the heat of the day, whiles away his time in carving fancied resemblances of human beings, of animals, and of natural objects. It is as common to the lover who, when waiting at the trysting place, passes his time in carving his own initials, or those of his lady-love, on a tree. To repeat Sir James Simpson's observation, man is at all times "a sculpturing and a painting animal."

Man, indeed, is the same in all climes, and is

instinctively led to do the same thing in the same way, under similar circumstances, in regions widely apart. As Humboldt remarks: "Nations of very different descent, when in a *similar uncivilized state* having the same disposition to simplify and generalize outlines, and being impelled, by inherent mental disposition, may be led *to produce similar signs and symbols.*" Hence we find identical forms in the carvings and sculpturings in countries the most remote from one another.

Identical circles with crosses within them are found carved on the cromlechs of Scandinavia, on the blocks forming an interior chamber of a tumulus at Dowth, in Ireland, on the rocks near Vernguas, Panama, and on the granite rocks near Arequipa, in Peru.

Identical concentric circles occur on the rocks at Lough Crew, in Ireland, and in Forsyth Co. Georgia, North America, as shown above.

These rude carvings cannot be considered as ornamentation, as their total want of symmetrical arrangement, and the absence of continuity in their repetition, preclude this.

Some of these traced figures may, however, be like the bomärke of the Scandinavians—private marks of property. The Red Indian had also his *totem*, the mark of his nation, and of the individual, and the

South Sea islander his peculiar *amoco*, or tattooed pattern. The mark discovered on a rock in the island of Bressay, Zetland, by Dr. Hunt, is evidently a Scandinavian bomärke. A mark on the rock of Masaya, in Nicaragua, seems to bear an analogy to this, and may be an Indian *totem*.

Catlin speaks, in his illustrations of the manners of the North American Indians, of thousands of inscriptions and paintings observed by him on the rocks near the Mississippi, whence the Indians got their red pipe stone. A Mandan Indian thus described their origin to him. "Many were the pipes we brought from thence, and we brought them in peace. We left our *totems* on the rocks, we cut them deep in the stones, they are there now."

Mr. Finn, in his "Byeways of Palestine," mentions that he observed upon various walls of dilapidated edifices at Ammân, curious marks slightly scratched, which almost resemble alphabetical characters, but are not, and which have, wherever met with, and wherever noticed, which is but seldom, puzzled travellers, however learned, to decipher. He copied the following :— (see p. 195).

These characters are tokens adopted by the Arabs to distinguish one tribe from another, and commonly used for branding the camels on the shoulders and

ON ROCK CARVINGS.

haunches, by which means the animals may be recovered, if straying and found by Arabs not hostile to the owners. In common parlance they are called the *Ausam* (plural of Wasam) of the several tribes. He further remarks that the presence of these rudely scratched Arab tribe-signs on edifices or tombs, show that persons of such tribes had visited there.

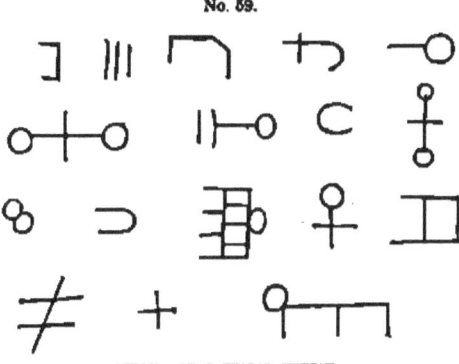

No. 59.

AUSAM—ARAB TRIBAL TOKENS.

Of a similar kind are the Bedouin marks, mentioned by Mr. Layard in his "Nineveh and Babylon," p. 309. "On some fragments of basaltic rock projecting from the summit of the cone (Kowkab) were numerous rudely cut signs, which might have been taken for ancient and unknown characters. They were the devices of the Shamman, carved there on the visit of different sheiks. Each tribe, and, indeed each subdivision and family, has its peculiar mark, to be placed upon their property, and burnt upon their camels."*

Carving these in idle moments, as we have already said, is as natural to the wild Arab, or the savage Indian, as to the idler of the present day, who carves his initials or monogram on a tree or bench.

Sir James Simpson has shown that most of these carvings belong to the stone age, which was synchronous with the pastoral phase of civilization. Some of a ruder description, like those noticed by Humboldt, in South America, may belong to an earlier age, or the hunting phase.

* M. De Sauley, who noticed them in the neighbourhood of the Dead Sea, calls them "Planetary Signs." According to Mr. E. H. Palmer ("Desert of the Exodus," p. 355)—"These tribe-marks consist in reality of distorted Himyaritic letters, generally the initial letter of the name; thus, the mark of the 'Anazch tribe is ☉, a circle with a dot in the centre, the ancient Himyaritic letter, 'Ain, with which the word 'Anazch begins. The Arabs themselves, being ignorant of writing, are of course unaware of this fact; they consequently designate their tribe-mark by the name of the article it may chance to resemble *ed dabbás*, "the club," *el báb*, "the door," and so on.

ADDENDUM.

Note to page 81. Pickering ("Races of Man") remarks that it is a mistake to suppose that the pastoral or nomadic life is a stage in the progressive improvement of society. Pastoral life is as much a stage in the development of man, as childhood is a stage in the development of the individual man; many individuals, however, remain in a state of childhood all their life, but this is the result of an arrested development, and of course *is* an abnormal state. In those widely extended regions, Scythia and Tartary, which Pickering mentions, where cultivation is impossible, all progress in development is necessarily checked.

INDEX.

ABORIGINES in Italy, 26; in India, Acorn, 155. [109.
Agricultural phase, 12; in Egypt, 23; in Western Asia, 24; in Greece, 25; in Italy, 25 ; in Ireland, 26; in England, 27; in France, 27; in Switzerland, 28; in Denmark, 28; in Germany, 29; in India, 31; in Mexico, 34; in Peru, 85.
Alignments, 161.
American Indians, 53, 68.
Ammán, 194.
Amoco, 194.
Analysis of bronze in Europe, Egypt, Mexico, Peru, gives nearly the same proportions, 98, 124.
Anderson, 6.
Arrow-heads, of flint, 53, 56, 102; of obsidian, 58, 69; of quartzite, 56, 69; of crystal, 62; of copper, 79; of bronze, 77; of iron, 96.
Aryans, 31, 107.
Australia, 153, 182.
Australians, 39, 41, 64, 70.
Ansam, Arab tribe-signs, 195.

Baker, Sir Samuel, 6.
Bally-hoo, 141.
Baring Gould, 12.

Barbarous phase, 9, 10, 17, 101; in England, 17; in France, 17; in Italy, 17, 19; in Sicily, 18; in Portugal, 19; in Denmark, 19; in Syria, 20; in India, 20; in America, 21; in Brazil, 21; in Peru, 22.
Barbed arrow, 57.
Barth, 150.
Bolcher, 50.
Bomärke, 193.
Brazil, 21.
Brehons, 127, 131.
Brehon law, 127.
Brett, 182.
Britons, 167.
Bronze age, 76, 106, 123.
Bronze, 76, 100; analysis of, 124; arrow-heads, spear-heads, 77; swords, 78. Greek, Roman, German, British, Irish swords, 79; implements, celts, 83.
Bulb of percussion, 48.

Camons, 108.
Capper, 169.
Capellini, 19.
Carved stones, Lough Crew, 177; carved rock, Forsyth Co. Georgia, 178.

INDEX.

Catlin, 59, 134.
Cat stones, 162.
Caves, 17, 19, 20, 21, 183, 184.
Celt, derivation of, 83.
Celts, stone, 61; copper, 73; bronze,
Celt mould, 91.   [83.
Chardin, 150.
Christy, 140, 184.
Circles, stone, 146, 151, 152, 153, 154; with crosses, 193; concentric, 193.
Classification of sepulchral monuments, 159; of flint and stone implements, 65.
Conwell, 176.
Copper, implements, 72, 75; hammered, 72; cast, 73.
Copper mines, 75.
Cores, 51.
Crannog, 175.
Croaghi, 140.
Cromlech, derivation of, 145.
Cromlechs, 140, 142; of the stone age, 162.
Cycle of development, 87.

Darab, 150.
Darwin, 19, 175.
Dawkins, Boyd, 18, 19.
Degraded phase, 87.
Dennis, 146, 172.
De Saulcy, 151, 196.
Desor, 68.
Dixon, 10.
Dodwell, 21, 190.
Dolmen, derivation of, 145.
Dolmen, Indian, 118.
Dowars, 138.
Du Noyer, 176.

Egypt, 22, 23, 52, 75.
Elliot, Sir Walter, 149.
Emilia, 108.
En amande, 43.
Enclosures, 137, 138.
Esquimaux, 50.
Evans, J., 43, 117, 118, 174.

Falconer, 18.
Fellahs, 88.
Fergusson, J., 33, 157, 158, 162, 165.
Figuier, 100.
Finlay, G., 51, 68, 75.
Finn, 194.
Finnè, 132.
Firbolgians, 26.
Flakes of flint, 45, 47, 51; of obsidian, 49, 51; of chert, 50, 51.
Flat celts of bronze, 83.
Flint flakes, 45, 51, chipped into shape, 59, 65.
Flint manufactories, 51, 52.
Flower, 150.
Foote, Bruce, 118.
Franks, A. W., 66, 79, 80, 91.
Friedrichshafen, 27, 104.

Gastaldi, 108.
Gibbon, 81.
Giotto, 187.
Greece, 25, 75.
Grossenhain, 108.
Guachos, 137.
Guiana, 182.

Hafting of stone hatchets, 63, 64; of bronze celts, 84.
Hallstadt, 95, 110.
Hamilton, 190.
Hazeroth, 138.

INDEX.

Herodotus, 22, 174.
Holed stones, 148.
Hooker, Dr., 147, 167.
Horace, 8.
Hovas, 167.
Humboldt, 7, 93, 178, 188, 193.
Hunt, Dr., 194.
Hunting phase, 8, 102; in Western Asia, 23; in Greece, 25; in Italy, 25; in Ireland, 26; in England, 27; in France, 27; in Switzerland, 28; in Denmark, 28; in Germany, 28; in India, 30; in Scythia, 31; in America, 31; Peru, 35.
Hut circles, of the pastoral age, 105.
Huxley, 170, 180.

Idleness of savages, 187.
Implements of the gravel drift, 41, 65, 118; stone, 60, 61, 104; bronze, 82, 104, 123; iron, 90, 111.
India, 20, 21.
Indented arrow-head, 56.
Intihuanas, sun-circles, 156.
Ireland, 26.
Ireland under the Brehon laws, 127.
Irish, early, 26, 168.
Irish celts, 62, 66.
Irish tribal system, 129, 131.
Iron age, 90, 111.

Jade, 67, 92.

Kasseum, 151.
Keller, 74, 117.
Khasia, 147, 167.
Kitchen-middens, 103, 174.
Koch, 21.

Lake Ballyhoe, 104.

Lake dwellings, 174.
Lamont, 152.
Land tenure in Ireland, 127.
Langues de chat, 41.
Law of sequence, 101.
Layard, 195.
Leaf-shaped arrow-head, 57.
Lepsius, 191.
Livingstone, 184.
Lough Crew, 176.
Lubbock, Sir John, 17, 40, 101, 107, 109, 112, 144.
Lund, 21.
Lukis, 172.
Lyell, Sir Charles, 3, 4, 110, 174.

Madden, Dr., 149.
Manco Capac, 35, 106.
Materials used for stone implements, Mario, 97, 111. [66.
Mayne Reid, Capt., 120.
Meadows Taylor, Col., 147.
Megalithic structures, 145, sepulchral, 153; not confined solely to non-Aryan races, 171.
Megalithic tomb, 153.
Mesolithic, 65.
Metal, importance of, 106.
Menhirs, 162.
Mexico, 84.
Mexicans, 84, 89, 90, 93.
Micali, 26.
Milesians, 26.
Millingen, 129.
Müller, Max, 31.
Mund, 136.

Natural state, 7.
Neolithic, 65.

INDEX.

Nephrite, 67, 68.
New Zealand, 69, 70.
Nilsson, 13, 16, 168, 185.

Obsidian, 49, 51, 58, 69.
Oliver, 149.
Osci, 25.

Pago, 21, 101.
Palæolithic, 63, 118.
Palgrave, F., 151.
Palmer, E. H., 138, 191, 196.
Palstaves of bronze, 83, 86, 125; of iron, 96.
Pastoral phase, 9, 105; in Egypt, 22; in Western Asia, 21; in Greece, 25; in Italy, 25; in Ireland, 26, 131, 141; in England, 27; in France, 27; in Switzerland, 28; in Germany, 29; in India, 30; in Scythia, 31; in America, 32; in Peru, 35.
Pelasgi, 25, 106.
Penrhyn Islands, 152.
Peru, 22, 35, 106, 154.
Peruvians, 34, 39, 75.
Poulvons, 162.
Phase, intermediate, 82; degraded, 87.
Phases, successive, in pre-historic times, 8; of civilization, earliest, 1; of civilization and contemporaneous implements, 99.
Piedra pintada, 179.
Pierres de tonnerre, 122.
Pre-historic phases, 1; barbarous phase, 5; hunting phase, 8; pastoral phase, 9; agricultural phase, 12.

Prescott, 32, 85, 93.
Pressigny, 52.
Primitive tomb, 155.
Progressive development of megalithic structures, 171.

Quartzite, 58.
Quetzalcoatl, 81, 106.

Raths, 136.
Rawlinson, 24.
Richey, 11.
Rock carvings, 170; of the pastoral age, 190.
Ross King, 13, 170.

Savage state—see barbarous phase.
Savage tribes, 5, 6, 7, 17, 19, 89.
Sequence of flint, stone, and bronze implements, 40.
Sequence of phases of civilization, 9; of phases of civilization and contemporaneous implements, 99.
Siculi, 25.
Simpson, Sir J., 164, 176, 184, 189, 196.
Sinaitic inscriptions, 190.
Smith, 26.
Socketed celts of bronze, 87, 88; of iron, 96.
Spear-heads of flint, 57; of bronze, 77; of iron, 96.
Squier, 75, 154, 156, 157, 168, 173, 179, 186.
Stage, transitional, copper, 71; from bronze to iron, 95, 110.
State of warfare, 116.
State of nature, 7.
Stemmed arrow-head, 56.

P

Stoddart, Sir John, 25.
Stone age, 56, 119, 122.
Stone circles, 146, 149, 153, 154; sepulchral, 159.
Stonehenge, 162; sepulchral, not a temple, 163.
Stone celts, 62.
Stone implements, 60, 61, 104; ground at edge, 59, 60; ground all over, 60, 61, 65.
Stuart, John, 160, 161.
Swords of bronze, 78; of iron, 95.
Symbolism, 186.

Tacitus, 29, 111.
Temples, 163.
Tennant, Sir E., 7.
Tenerife, 69.
Tiahuanaco, 155.
Tierra del Fuego, 19, 175.
Todas, 136, 170.
Tomb, 158, 155.
Toom Castle, 104.
Toosl, 186.
Totem, 193, 194.
Transition period, copper, 71; from bronze to iron, 95, 110.
Triangular arrow-head, 56.
Tribe, 10, 129.

Tribal system, 10, 129; in Ireland, 131.
Tribal tokens or signs, 195.
Trilithon, 162.
Tristam, H., 20.
Tuath de Danaans, 26, 106.
Tumulus, 144.
Tunja, 157.
Tylor, E., 58, 72, 94, 148.

Usher, 128.

Veddahs, 6.
Vogüé, Count de, 191.

Waitz, 1.
Whately, Arch., 7.
Wilkinson, Sir Gardner, 15, 23.
Wilson, Dr., 2, 41, 129, 166.
Wilson, Captain, 151.
Wilde, Sir W., 26, 27, 49, 56, 61, 67, 73, 74, 83, 123.
Winged celt, 84, 85, 86.
Woky hole, 18.
Wolds, Yorkshire, 103.
Worsaae, 28, 107, 122.

Yorkshire Wolds, 103.

www.ingramcontent.com/pod-product-compliance
Lightning Source LLC
Chambersburg PA
CBHW021831230426
43669CB00008B/930